Gilles Deleuze

Titles in the series Critical Lives present the work of leading cultural figures of the modern period. Each book explores the life of the artist, writer, philosopher or architect in question and relates it to their major works.

In the same series

Gilles Deleuze

Frida Beckman

REAKTION BOOKS

To Julia and Logan – this one too is for you

Published by
REAKTION BOOKS LTD
Unit 32, Waterside
44–48 Wharf Road
London N1 7UX, UK

www.reaktionbooks.co.uk

First published 2017

Printed and bound in Great Britain by Bell & Bain, Glasgow

A catalogue record for this book is available from the British Library

ISBN 978 1 78023 731 2

Contents

Gilles Deleuze in 1986.

Prologue

> In life there is a sort of awkwardness, a delicacy of health, a frailty
> of constitution, a vital stammering which is someone's charm.
> Charm is the source of life just as style is the source of writing.[1]

Gilles Deleuze had a rather determined disinterest in the life of the
author. Or, to qualify this somewhat, the lives of authors, at least as
supposed mirrors to their work, rarely seemed relevant for Deleuze.
And he is far from alone in this disinterest. Look, for example, at
how one of the most influential Continental philosophers of the
twentieth century, Martin Heidegger, summarizes and thereby
dismisses the biography of Aristotle, one of the most influential
philosophers of all time: 'He was born, he thought, he died.' Like
many philosophers, Heidegger considered the life of the philosopher
as little but anecdotal. In his case, this approach is also slightly
ironic considering the way in which his own involvement with the
Nazis during the Second World War has prompted a revaluation
of any easy dismissals of the relevance of a philosopher's life. What
is particularly interesting to note in that context is that although
the international research community was already well aware
of Heidegger's Nazi sympathies, the publication of his 'Black
Notebooks' in 2014 pressed this community to consider the idea
that Heidegger's political convictions were a stain not only on his
career and person but on his philosophy. In the light of the
notebooks, which point to the profoundness of his anti-Semitism,

the possibility of separating a philosopher's life and work is put into crisis. This crisis makes it necessary to ask if it is possible to maintain the conviction, as did Hannah Arendt, that in reading philosophers like Plato or Heidegger it ultimately does not matter 'where the storms of their century may have driven them', because their thinking emerges not from their historical context but from some eternal abode in which all remains perfect.[2]

What these concerns indicate is how the idea of an immaculately conceived philosophical thinking separated from the messiness of embodied life persists in what has been largely a male philosophical tradition. Female philosophers have rarely been allowed this disembodied perfection. Indeed, the attention given to Arendt herself as a person and subsequent generations' fascination with her brief relationship with Heidegger constitute a prime example of the attention more frequently given to the personal and embodied lives of female thinkers. But of course, there are also those who question this separation between life and work. Friedrich Nietzsche remarked at one point that it had gradually occurred to him 'what every great philosophy has been so far: namely the personal confession of its author and a kind of involuntary and unnoticed *mémoires.*'[3] Jacques Derrida cites Heidegger's dismissal of Aristotle's biography not to support but to disclaim it, and suggests that we need to rethink the exclusion of a writer's life 'as a corpus of empirical accidents'. Philosophers' biographies, he argues, must be put 'back into the picture'. Their political convictions are particularly important in Derrida's view, but so too are their embodied lives more generally: 'Why do philosophers present themselves in their work as asexual beings? Why have they effaced their private lives from their work?'[4] What Derrida speaks for is not some direct translation between an author's life and work, as if the former could explain the latter, but the impossibility of thinking pure text, that is, a text without traces. After the death of the author, officially declared by Roland Barthes and further deliberated on by Michel Foucault in the late 1960s, it is also increasingly uncommon to draw direct parallels between author and text. The writer, Barthes insists, does not precede or exceed the writing, but is born with it. This is not a birth that happens once but one that happens at every reading. And because the text emerges from a tissue of already existing texts, the author is not so much expressing '*himself*' as he is providing a particular assembly of and encounter between components. Therefore, giving a text an author 'is to impose a limit on that text, to furnish it with a final signified, to close the writing.'[5]

In the case of Deleuze, it speaks not just against his views on the life of the author but against his philosophy as a whole to focus on and give a chronological account of a life, an account that defines and inevitably delimits all the things that it expressed. Such a process 'closes down' life by giving it a limit, a shape, a final signified in the form of a defined individual and a delimited life story. And yet, here we are, eager to know a little bit more than the fact that Deleuze was born and that he thought and that he died. Before accepting the invitation to write this book, I struggled with a number of caveats, four of which seem particularly relevant. The first and most central is Deleuze's own fundamental scepticism towards the individual as a given unity. Of course, I could settle for writing a history of the individual. Indeed, this is what is done all the time, not the least in our present genre of biography. Frequently, such biographies rely on a set of starting points that they do not always find necessary to problematize, such as, most centrally, notions of the individual, the body, temporality and history. As such, they implicitly perpetuate certain preconceptions about what constitute the basic components of life as well as the relation between them. Such preconceptions may be quite functional, and they certainly make it easier for the writers and readers of such biographies to immediately recognize the units and logics at hand. Biographies of philosophers, however, are a somewhat particular case, as I have already noted, as philosophy's identification with its most famous names runs parallel with the sense that the lives of these philosophers are irrelevant to the understanding of their thought. And while there is a lingering sense that there may be some connection between the life of philosophers and their thinking, as Peter Osborne notes, it is rare to find biographies that manage to deliver a reflexive and satisfactory account of this connection.[6] In striving to provide such a reflexive and satisfactory account, and thus to write a biography of Deleuze that in some way also reflects his philosophy, I cannot, or at least definitely should not, fall back on preconceptions about the individual, the body, temporality and history. Moreover, the idea of capturing a life and drawing it into a linear narrative, of focusing on 'man', of thinking that we could somehow organize, understand and 'know' life according to chronological structures, is a project that Deleuze himself would vehemently resist.

The second and not inconsiderable qualification is the already existing 650-page biography of Deleuze and his oft-co-writer Félix Guattari. While this study, François Dosse's *Gilles Deleuze et Félix Guattari: Biographie croisée* (2007; *Gilles Deleuze and Félix Guattari: Intersecting Lives*, 2010), has been the subject of some critique, any readers hungry for details about Deleuze's life could treat themselves to considerable helpings from this source. However, there are many differences between Dosse's extensive biography and the present one – they are different not only in scope but in methodology, goal and conviction – including two to which I would like to pay special attention, as they are central to understanding the ambitions and limitations of the present project. A first and obvious difference between them is, of course, that the former is equally preoccupied with both Deleuze's and Guattari's lives, while the present one focuses only on Deleuze's. Dosse's attention to Guattari is important on many levels, as he has often been placed in the shadow of Deleuze. In critical discourse, a reference to

Deleuze frequently turns out to be a reference to their joint work. This tendency is not limited to a post-Deleuzo-Guattarian context but was noted by Deleuze himself in the 1970s: as he writes in a letter to Guattari, 'people erase you and abstractify me'.[7] While this tendency persists today, the work of Guattari is currently gaining focus in its own right. Gary Genosko has been a central figure in this context, having worked since the mid-1990s to underline and bring out the importance of Guattari's work. Dosse's book may fit in well with what Osborne calls 'the emergent, second state in the reception of Deleuze-and-Guattari: Guattari studies, or what the philosopher Eric Alliez has called "the Guattari-Deleuze effect".'[8] The attention to Guattari, in other words, is most welcome.

The second important difference between Dosse's biography and mine is that large parts of his study are built on interview material, both his own and others', which allows him to present detailed accounts of many different life events. This makes for a richly detailed dual biography of great interest to many and, as you will see, I will repeatedly point readers in its direction for more detailed accounts of various events in Deleuze's life.[9] Indeed, some readers may choose, at this point, to revert to that study. For the one you presently hold in your hand, such attention to detail is not only beyond the possible in terms of space, but is also beyond the desirable in terms of how it hopes to situate Deleuze's life and work in a critical, reflexive discussion that also tries to grapple with the philosophical hesitation of pursuing such a project in the first place.[10]

A third concern with writing this biography is my acute awareness of the many scholars engaging with Deleuze's work and who know his work very well, and who will no doubt note details I left out and also the things I included, possibly critically. Within the framework of this kind of book there is no way I can accommodate all his readers and all the nuances of the life and philosophy that we associate with Deleuze. A book of this brevity cannot aim to cover all Deleuze's concepts – for indeed, there are many. Instead, I will focus on those that seem to create the most productive connections with the various dimensions of his life. In trying to locate the most fruitful connections between Deleuze's life and work, I decided to let myself be guided by one of his own concepts.[11] The concept of the assemblage (*agencement*) is developed by Deleuze and Guattari to help them rethink the notion of the individual. A statement is never individual, they argue, but always collective. Forces, bodies, objects and territories form temporary assemblages fuelled by desire and with a particular function. These forces form an assemblage when its set of components becomes machinic. The notion of the machinic is important because it indicates that the assemblage is active while stressing its nonpersonal and nonhuman dimension. It functions not because of an individual but because of a combination of movements. Thus, Deleuze and Guattari explain, the assemblage has two sides: 'it is a collective assemblage of enunciation; it is a machinic assemblage of desire.'[12] The concept of the assemblage resists the idea of the individual or personal and suggests that a statement, rather than referring back to a subject, 'occurs necessarily as a function of a national, political, and social community'.[13]

If we approach Deleuze's biography in order to delineate how components of his life and work emerge and are part of larger assemblages with collective functions, then we may be able to provide an account of his life that is also, at least to some extent, illustrative of his philosophy. There is a way, Deleuze argues, of using a name, not to denote an ego or person or subject, but as a denotation of the intensities and multiplicities that run through an individual. This is not the depersonalization of the history of philosophy that builds on subjection, but a depersonalization that builds on love as it recognizes the 'singularities, words, names, fingernails, things, animals, little events' that are gathered under this name.[14] By focusing on a set of forces, objects, bodies and territories, it may be possible to locate functioning assemblages, their temporalities and the desires that fuel them, as well as how they have occurred, and keep occurring, around the life and work of Deleuze. Accordingly, then, this book will be divided into a number of assemblages. Bookended by a chapter on his early life, A Child, and his death, A Life, the three middle chapters – An Apprenticeship, A Friendship and A Practice – follow three periods in his work: a first one in which he mainly writes on earlier philosophers, a second characterized by collaborative projects, mainly with Guattari, and a third in which he writes on art and cinema. The singular form in the title of each chapter is quite purposeful. It functions to underline how the parts of Deleuze's private and intellectual life outlined in each section are singular points in a larger context.

My final worry pertains to the claims I hereby make on a life – a life that I can only partly know and exclusively from secondary sources, a life that was cherished by his family and friends who will always know more and different things from those that can be catalogued here. Therefore, I want to stress that this critical biography is just that – it is not the kind of biography based on interviews with friends and family intended to unbury all the details of a writer's life, but rather a critical effort that endeavours to illuminate some fruitful dialogues between Deleuze's life and work. And indeed, there is something slightly twisted about writing a biography of Deleuze, as a whole set of aspects of such a project speak against the philosophy that we would thus attempt to 'close' – in Barthes' words – or 'capture', as Deleuze himself might have phrased it. Maybe this is exactly why the project intrigued me. I took it as a challenge to locate that 'room for play' which, as Jacques Rancière puts it, emerges when we try to understand a thinker, not by striving 'to coincide with his center' but by 'leading him on a trajectory where his articulations come undone', creating that foreign-language-within-a-language that Deleuze himself

Deleuze: creation, encounters, becomings. Graffiti portrait in Houmt Souk, Tunisia.

strove for.[15] I have tried to enable that room for play by taking inspiration from Eleanor Kaufman's argument that working with Deleuze must be an act of 'betraying well'. As Kaufman points out, another perverse but surprisingly frequent way of approaching Deleuze's work is by means of a loyal reading of his texts and a faithful application of his concepts that, too, speaks fundamentally against his philosophy.[16] For Deleuze, following too closely in another's footsteps means closing the door on what both life and philosophy are supposed to be about: creation, encounters, becomings. So, ideally then, this critical biography, in noting that Deleuze's thinking did not emerge from an eternal abode in which all is perfect, should pay attention to such creations, encounters and becomings. Deleuze was very much, and very painfully, embodied, and he was born, again and again, along with texts, with encounters and with friendships. This is what I hope to provide here – less a chronicle of his life or a 'final signifier' to close the writing and more a mapping of the encounters through which we can see him and his thinking emerge.

1
A Child

Doing literature by calling upon childhood, it's typically to make literature into one's tiny private affair, it's totally disgusting . . . truly shit . . . so, the task of the writer is not to go digging through the family archives . . . Our task is to become child through writing, reach a childhood of the world, restore a childhood of the world. That's the task of literature.[1]

Gilles Deleuze's life was, it has frequently been pointed out, unremarkable. He was born on 18 January 1925 in the 7th arrondissement in Paris. Here, he came to spend most of his life, exempting brief periods in his youth. He was the son of the conservative, right-wing engineer Louis Deleuze and housewife Odette Camaüer who, Deleuze recounts, found it impossible to share the beaches in Normandy with working-class people, or, as he recalls her putting it, with people 'like that'.[2] Deleuze played tennis until he was fourteen but stopped at the onset of the Second World War in 1939. When the war reached France in 1940, the family was on holiday in Normandy. Deleuze was fifteen years old at the time and his parents decided to leave him and his older brother Georges in Normandy, where they ended up staying in a *pension* and attending school for a year. Whether he found the mere mention of it unbearable or whether he rejected it as irrelevant, Deleuze did not find discussions of his childhood very rewarding.

In order to comprehend this point and thus begin to get to know Deleuze, we may interrogate the tension between unbearable and irrelevant, a tension that is, after all, considerable. In his biography, Dosse detects two major reasons for Deleuze's rejection of his own childhood. The first is the fact that his parents were bourgeois, 'de droite' and uncultivated, which did not make for a sense of belonging. In fact, and although Deleuze was not as actively political as many of his friends and fellow philosophers in the 1960s, the conservative and reactionary politics that his parents stood for was to become the implicit and sometimes explicit target of his future philosophy. The second reason is that Deleuze grew up in the shadow of his dead brother. Georges, who fought in the Résistance during the war, was caught by the Germans and died on his way to a concentration camp. Georges became the worshipped hero compared to whom Gilles would never be able to shine. Although Deleuze came to dismiss this later, he once told his friend the novelist Michel Tournier that he could never forgive his parents for this betrayal. This absent brother, Dosse notes, thus came to play a significant role in the shaping of Deleuze's childhood.[3] And indeed, it is not hard to imagine that a child who not only loses a sibling but who is also made to feel insignificant in his shadow finds the mention of their childhood unbearable. But to say that this childhood is irrelevant is a different thing altogether. Why would Deleuze do that?

The emphasis here should not be on the notion of 'childhood' itself but on the idea of one's 'own' childhood. The child stands for a largely constructive function in Deleuze's philosophy. It recurs in various places in his writing and also performs different functions, not all of which, it has been noted, are purely positive.[4] A child is vulnerable and exposed but a recurring dimension that Deleuze returns to is the child as that which is not yet fully incorporated into stable, or molar, structures. A molar construction for Deleuze is the opposite of becoming, as it implies a construction that has received well-defined boundaries.[5] Becoming, in turn, is a key concept in Deleuze's philosophy, and he uses it to shift the focus from being, as a fixed starting or ending point, to becoming, as the process of life itself. Rather than thinking of being as a goal towards which a process of becoming aims, Deleuze emphasizes becoming itself as the primary condition of all life. This way, the emphasis comes to fall on temporary organizations in a world of constant flux and difference. The flux and difference are more apparent in the figure of the child, but the adult world soon comes to overcode with its molar structures what is essentially an experimental body, sexuality and subjectivity. The figure of the child thus harbours the potential of deterritorializing, or unsettling, the ingrained structures of adulthood. Deterritorialization, an important term for Deleuze, especially in his work with Guattari, is essentially about freeing up territorialized – that is, more fixed – bodies, spaces or relations, in order to display the differences that they see as inherent in them. The child itself thus has a productive function, the function of helping us recognize the impersonal and creative dimensions of life.

A writer, or a biographer, who reconstructs childhood memories and events is likely to project a molar logic onto that which was not yet molar. The experimental thus comes to be claimed and domesticized into that which is no longer experimental. We lose sight of becoming. Therefore, writing should not be an individual affair, not a return to one's own childhood. For Deleuze, such writing mutilates life, debases and mortifies it. Rather, writing should be about becoming – 'becoming anything but a writer'.[6] For such a becoming to be possible, you must write yourself out of, not into, neurosis. To do so, you may want to write about *a* childhood but not *your* childhood. Making writing into a becoming-child, the experimental is allowed back into our lives and room is created for experimentation and becoming. This means writing oneself out of, not into, the structures that have

seemingly determined identity. This is also why we must qualify
Dosse's explanation of Deleuze's rejection of his childhood and,
indeed, the familial altogether – an aspect of his philosophy that
we will discuss further in Chapter Three – as directly linked to
his own childhood and family experience. A too directly personal
account of his childhood and the familial delimits our possibilities
of understanding not just Deleuze's life, but the mechanisms of his
contemporaneity more broadly. If we choose to see his critique of
the familial primarily in the light of the fact that his own childhood
was difficult, we remain blind to the larger social, political and
philosophical dimensions of constructions of childhood and the
family. We also fail to see the many other machinic assemblages
that make up a childhood. We need not look further than to one of
Deleuze's first sources of inspiration, the young literature professor
Pierre Halbwachs, to see how an understanding of the familial is
insufficient.

Until his time in Normandy, Deleuze recounts in *L'Abécédaire
de Gilles Deleuze*, a series of televised interviews with Claire Parnet
filmed in 1988–9, he had been a bored young man and a middling
student. But this break with his routines and his encounter with
Halbwachs, whose failing health had kept him out of the war,
was the starting point of the intellectual curiosity that came to
characterize Deleuze's life from then on.[7] Halbwachs was the son
of the influential sociologist and philosopher Maurice Halbwachs,
who was captured by the Gestapo and died in Buchenwald. We
may make a preliminary note here of what will be explored later:
the links of war, friendship, illness, health and literature that were
present in these early phases of Deleuze's life. And while we are still
here, at the sand dunes of Normandy where Deleuze walked with
his friend, we may also want to note that his first intellectual sparks
were kindled by literature rather than philosophy. While Deleuze
was clearly not a literary scholar, his philosophical thinking was
to be much influenced by literature and his literary references

almost run parallel to the philosophical ones.[8] What came to be particular about his approach to literature, and to which we will return in Chapter Four, was that he did not see literary texts as representations of life so much as active dimensions of it. Perhaps his exchanges with Halbwachs in Normandy – an exchange so intense that a worried landlady tried to warn both Deleuze and his parents of Halbwachs's supposed pederast tendencies – contributed to a philosophy in which literature and life cannot be separated.

It did not take long, however, until Deleuze's attraction to literature was outshone by a fascination with philosophy. After the Armistice, he left Normandy and returned to Paris. Here, his early years of high school took place in the shadow of the occupation but also illuminated by the friends and professors who contributed towards his discovery and passion for what was to become his future vocation. Deleuze describes taking philosophy classes with one Monsieur Vialle as the beginnings of his instant and lifelong love for philosophy: 'When I learned of the existence, that there were such strange things called "concepts", that had the same effect on me as, for some other people, the encounter with characters from a magnificent novel.' If Halbwachs was one early source of inspiration, Monsieur Vialle certainly was another. Deleuze recounts how they used to walk to school and back together, talking incessantly. 'Halbwachs had helped me learn something about what literature was, yet from my very first classes in philosophy, I knew this is what I would do.'[9] Important as this introduction to philosophy was to Deleuze, it is interesting to note that he was assigned to Vialle's class by chance and that the other philosophy class at the Lycée Carnot at the time was taught by Maurice Merleau-Ponty. One can only wonder how being introduced to philosophy by the latter instead might have influenced the young Deleuze.

Three central aspects colour accounts of Deleuze's early years as an academic – from the final year of high school to his subsequent studies in philosophy at the Sorbonne. The first is a sharp intelligence that makes those around him recognize him as exceptional. His friend Tournier describes how he, while claiming some credit for introducing Deleuze to philosophy by bringing him to his philosophy class, soon saw him soar. Tournier recalls that while he and his fellow pupils tossed arguments back and forth among themselves 'like balls of cotton or rubber', Deleuze's arguments came hurled at them more in the shape of 'iron and steel cannonballs'. 'We soon', he writes, 'came to fear his talent for seizing upon a single one of our words and using it to expose our banality, stupidity, or failure of intelligence.'[10] Still, and despite this depiction of Deleuze as a rather awe-inspiring character, Tournier also accounts for how Deleuze became the inspirational centre for this group of young students:

> Anyone who has never known such a feverish need to delve deeply, to think systematically and use one's own mind to the full, who has never experienced such a frenzied passion for the absolute, will I fear never know quite what thinking means.[11]

Through Tournier, who had in turn been invited by his teacher Maurice de Gandillac, Deleuze had the opportunity to attend the gatherings at Marie-Magdeleine Davy's estate outside Paris, where she hosted many cultural and politically coloured events. There Deleuze, who was still in high school, had the opportunity to spend time with established writers and philosophers such as Pierre Klossowski, Jean Paulhan, Georges Bataille and Jean-Paul Sartre.

The second trait outlined in accounts of the young Deleuze is his confidence and audacity in this kind of context. He seemed little concerned with disciplinary hierarchies or philosophical traditions. Dosse describes how Deleuze took every opportunity to talk philosophy with his professors and, while himself just a senior in high school, seemed perfectly at ease discussing Nietzsche with

Klossowski, who was twenty years his senior.[12] In another context, fellow student and subsequently lifelong friend François Châtelet recalls how Deleuze, assigned to perform a reading before a most serious and meticulous historian of philosophy, delivered such an audacious but ultimately brilliant reading that it took the teacher through all the stages from paling to incredulity to admiration.[13]

A third trait that seems to have been apparent even during these early years is Deleuze's aspiration to reinvent thinking. He was impatient with the way the history of philosophy seemed to restrict rather than encourage independent thinking and found the milieu at the Sorbonne claustrophobic. 'I belong to a generation,' he said, 'one of the last generations, that was more or less bludgeoned to death with the history of philosophy.'[14] But even as a student, it was clear that Deleuze would not let himself be smothered by tradition. He had, Tournier recalls, astonishing powers of rearrangement, which entailed that 'all the tired philosophy of the curriculum passed through him and emerged unrecognizable but rejuvenated, with a fresh, undigested, bitter taste of newness that we weaker, lazier minds found disconcerting and repulsive.'[15] And as those familiar with how his work panned out can testify, Deleuze continued on this path of the slightly disconcerting. He never allowed himself to be 'bludgeoned to death' but rather developed a joy in doing philosophy well beyond any straitjacket of tradition. As fellow philosopher Michel Serres was to say about Deleuze much later: 'The greatest praise I can give to him is to say that philosophical thinking made him truly happy, profoundly serene.'[16]

In these early years we can also find a number of clues to who and what influenced Deleuze. Although he was later to distance himself from him and from phenomenology more generally, the young Deleuze was clearly both influenced and inspired by Sartre. In the context of a suffocating tradition, the work of Sartre came to inspire Deleuze, as it did many others of his generation.

To Tournier and the group of students to which he and Deleuze belonged, Sartre's *Being and Nothingness* arrived like a meteor: 'we had the extraordinary good fortune of seeing a philosophy born before our very eyes.'[17] Deleuze, as we have already seen, had been hungry for thinking that exceeded tradition – and here it was. 'Who', he wrote in a tribute to Sartre after the latter had refused the Nobel Prize for Literature in 1964, 'except Sartre knew how to say anything new?'[18] He describes the first performances of Sartre's *The Flies*, the publication of *Being and Nothingness* (both in 1943) and the presentation 'Existentialism is a Humanism' at the Club Maintenant in 1945 as 'events: they were how we learned, after long nights, the identity of thought and life.'[19] Indeed, Deleuze's very first official publication, in 1945 at the age of twenty, was to be a pastiche on Sartre entitled 'Description of Woman: For a Philosophy of the Sexed Other'.[20]

There is work from this early period that Deleuze requested be removed from his official bibliography and which has therefore been largely neglected until recently. If Sartre was the name of the day, Deleuze also went 'potholing', as Christian Kerslake puts it, 'in a number of obscure places, out of sight of the daylight concerns of his culture and times.'[21] Some of these, such as Henri Bergson's work on instinct and memory, were later to become central features of Deleuze's work, but there are many others that have remained in the shadows. Kerslake mentions Jungianism, the esotericism of Johann Malfatti von Monteregio and Jósef Maria Hoëne-Wronski, and Ludwig Binswanger on schizophrenia, sorcery, drug experimentation – all people, and subjects, of which pertained to working towards a theory of the unconscious that recovers dimensions of it that Freudian theories had occluded.[22] It is quite possible, Joshua Ramey suggests, that Deleuze picked up this interest in Davy's salons. Davy herself was a 'passionate spiritualist' and there were both esotericists and occultists present at these gatherings.[23] In his early twenties, Deleuze was invited, possibly via Davy, to write a preface to a French translation of the work of Malfatti, who was a highly influential esotericist in his own time of the nineteenth century but whose work had since become increasingly obscure. But, along with other essays, this text on Malfatti was part of the material Deleuze later wanted to remove.[24] This work, published by the small French press Griffon d'Or in 1946, shows that he, at this stage, was attracted to Malfatti's perception of *mathesis* as a way of understanding the relation between individuality and the universal as inseparable.

Malfatti's name never recurs in Deleuze's work and it may be tempting, therefore, to think of this early work as 'a youthful dalliance with the occult'. But although many of these early writers and theories do not appear by name, Kerslake notes occult themes recurring throughout Deleuze's writing.[25] An awareness of these influences on Deleuze's thinking explains and illuminates many aspects of his later work. His later theories of immanence can be given more nuance with an awareness of the esoteric knowledge he picked up in these early years, as Ramey notes,[26] and Deleuze and Guattari's references to sorcery and implicit rehabilitation of the occult in *Mille plateaux* (1980; *A Thousand Plateaus*, 1987) can be better understood through an awareness of Deleuze's early writing on Malfatti and the occult.[27] Similarly, Deleuze's discussions of the unconscious in *Différence et répétition* (1968; *Difference and Repetition*, 1994) may make more sense when we read Jung into the equation,[28] and it may also be interesting to investigate how Jungian principles influenced Deleuze's early essay on masochism as well as Deleuze and Guattari's later work on freeing sexuality and desire from the hooks of psychoanalysis.[29]

Looking back at these early stages of Deleuze's life, from his childhood to his entry into philosophy, we must take care not to draw oversimplified lines between childhood events, early influences and writing. Consulting Deleuze's own conception of memory, which is largely influenced by the work of Bergson, we are reminded not to construct an individual, linear history and insist on a superficial and limiting causality in the face of a much richer and multi-layered existence. 'Memory', Deleuze writes in one of his *Cinéma* books, 'is not in us; it is we who move in a Being-memory, a world-memory.'[30] Memory may seem to be chronological – 'It is true that these regions (my childhood, my adolescence, my adult life, etc.), appear to succeed each other' – but the past is really just 'a past in general; the coexistence of all the sheets of past'. Here he recruits the Italian film director Federico Fellini to his cause: 'What Fellini says is Bergsonian: "We are constructed in memory; we are *simultaneously* childhood, adolescence, old age, and maturity."'[31] For Deleuze, then, time is not chronological and the past exists as sheets, or circles that dilate or contract in relation to the present. In the present, our subjectivity is produced precisely in the process of perceiving, or remembering, repetitions in the fabric of difference. There is, as we will see, no such thing as the repetition of the same, according to Deleuze, but memory is the function that nonetheless helps us to construct a sense of continuity. Memory thereby harbours both an enabling and a limiting function. It is the condition that enables a sense of selfhood but it is also what risks closing down our potential for becoming. The risk is such mainly if we see history – be it our personal or a larger history – as a strictly chronological narrative. In so doing, our subjectivity is locked into a linear trajectory from which we may not be able to escape: 'My childhood was like that, therefore I am now like this.' If we recognize the nonlinear sheets of the past as circles, on the other hand, memory, and thus also subjectivity, is kept open to different, and differential, trajectories. Only in forgetting memories, as we thought we knew them, can we break free from delimiting structures. Your childhood is not your childhood. You are a child of the world. The aim is 'becoming the child of one's own events'.[32]

So if I asked in the introductory chapter how we are to 'know' Deleuze, I feel the need to ask, in this one, how we are to 'forget' him in a productive way. This is not forgetting as in repudiating – it is not the forgetting of Foucault that Baudrillard once called for – but as in realizing that a rather important part of the project of understanding Deleuze's life and work must be to see that we see nothing if we try to pin them down too narrowly.[33] Indeed, and as we will see through the rest of this book, much of Deleuze's own work revolved around unpinning such understandings. An active forgetting, such as the one Nietzsche outlines in his *On the Genealogy of Morals* (1887) and with which Deleuze was no doubt familiar, constitutes a 'positive faculty of repression' and brings with it health, by making room for the present and for the new. Active forgetting is an antidote to an identity that binds the future to the past and the present in causal chains.[34] Letting thinking fold and unfold through apprenticeships, friendships and practices was a way for Deleuze to forget himself, of creating spaces for thought that are not delimited by the enclosures of chronological and personal memory but that rather affirm memory outside the forceful framework of the habitual repetition that is subjectivity.

Ultimately, a Deleuzian conception of childhood demands that we turn Freudian theory on its head. The unconscious is not about repressed memories or phantasms that a sufficiently skilful psychoanalysis can draw out; it is something that is produced in the present. 'The unconscious is a substance to be manufactured, to get flowing – a social and political space to be conquered.' For the same reason, childhood memories are not reproduced but are part of a becoming-child of the present, a raw material from which various assemblages may be constructed.[35] Again, we can hear the echo of Nietzsche here, as he speaks, in *Thus Spoke Zarathustra* (1883–91), of what the child can do that neither the camel nor the lion can: the child offers a forgetfulness and a new beginning that affirms life as true creation.[36] We may conclude, then, in a most preliminary fashion, that while the child, or rather a child, is an important concept for Deleuze, it cannot for him be his own childhood that matters, but rather 'the childhood of the world'. In the end, Deleuze agrees that he was *a child*. The indefinite article here is crucial. It has, as he says, 'extreme richness', and in a sense a critical biography of Deleuze should be a biography of this indefinite article. It starts with a child.

2
An Apprenticeship

> I suppose the main way I coped with it at the time was to see the
> history of philosophy as a sort of buggery or (it comes to the same
> thing) immaculate conception. I saw myself as taking an author
> from behind and giving him a child that would be his own offspring,
> yet monstrous.[1]

After passing his *agrégation* in 1948, which meant the end of his
university studies and the granting of a teaching certificate,[2]
Deleuze had the choice of many different possible ways ahead.
He could, Giuseppe Bianco points out, have aimed for a career in
the social sciences and humanities, as did fellow student Michel
Foucault, or for one in epistemology, as did Gilbert Simondon,
or in phenomenology, as did Jacques Derrida and Jean-François
Lyotard. Instead, and like Louis Althusser and François Châtelet,
he chose to focus on the history of philosophy.[3] During this period,
from the 1940s onwards, historians of philosophy were, as Bianco
notes, questioning their role within institutions as well as the
epistemological status of their entire discipline. The influence
of German history, theories of Marxism and the emergence of a
sociology of knowledge are some of the reasons listed by Bianco to
explain why these philosophers felt the need to revisit the function
and borders of their discipline. Deleuze's original contribution
to philosophy emerges at least in part from these tensions. His
profound interest in the history of philosophy is accompanied by

a desire to free thinking from the humanist idea of the philosopher himself as being at the centre of this history.[4]

And as we began to see in the previous chapter, early on Deleuze developed a disrespect for tradition that was both productive and affirmative: 'The history of philosophy', he argues, 'plays a patently repressive role in philosophy.'[5] It is a 'formidable school of intimidation which manufactures specialists in thought – but which also makes those who stay outside conform all the more to this specialism which they despise. An image of thought called philosophy has been formed historically and it effectively stops people from thinking.'[6] These rather unforgiving words on the role of the history of philosophy are not, however, reflected in Deleuze's personal relationships with the historians of philosophy of the time. He highly respected and was also respected by Sorbonne philosophers such as Martial Gueroult, Ferdinand Alquié, Maurice de Gandillac and Jean Wahl, and maintained friendships with many of them through his life. It is important to note, as does Alan D. Schrift, that while Deleuze now seems so contemporary, he also enjoyed this mutual respect with some of the most academically mainstream philosophers of his own period. Neither are Deleuze's seemingly harsh words mirrored in the works on the history of philosophy that he ultimately came to write, all of which, Schrift points out, are characterized by affirmation and generosity.[7] Indeed, Deleuze keenly hoped that the philosophers he wrote on would have experienced joy had they been able to read his work.

If Deleuze's severe words on the history of philosophy are not to be taken as a reflection on his personal relationships, neither are they mirrored in any sort of repudiation or avoidance of this history. Indeed, his early work developed around the work of a set of earlier philosophers. His first published book was on David Hume – *Empirisme et subjectivité* (*Empiricism and Subjectivity*) in 1953 – after which followed books on Nietzsche, Immanuel Kant, Bergson and Baruch Spinoza (and, much later, Michel Foucault and Gottfried Wilhelm Leibniz).[8] This line-up of books on earlier philosophers that characterizes Deleuze's early work may seem to speak against the idea of breaking free from predetermined routes of thinking which remained so central throughout his life. This seeming contradiction is further underlined by the fact that the names of the philosophers he worked on at this stage also coincide to a large extent with the philosophers whose work had been taught at university, as Dosse points out. Jean Hyppolite, the supervisor of Deleuze's first dissertation, gave lectures on Hume in 1946–7, on Kant in 1947–8 and on Bergson in 1948–9; Alquié, who was the supervisor of his minor thesis on Spinoza, gave classes on Spinoza in 1958–9; and Wahl, who remained an important influence on Deleuze, gave courses on Nietzsche between 1958 and '61.[9] Furthermore, and as Schrift notes, many of the philosophers Deleuze would end up working on, such as Bergson, Kant, Spinoza, Nietzsche, Hume and the Stoics, were on the reading list for the *agrégation de philosophie* during the late 1950s, when Deleuze was at the Sorbonne.[10] This influential list, which stipulates obligatory reading for students aiming to pass this exam and thus qualify to teach, also has great weight when it comes to which philosophers are taught in university courses in the field – and thus has considerable impact on the field as a whole in its French context.[11] At one point, Deleuze describes this attention to the philosophers already at hand as an act of initiation. Like Van Gogh or Gauguin, he suggests, you have to keep painting portraits for a long time before you can move on to doing your own landscapes, and, like them, it might take a while before you dare use the stronger colours. This is an exercise not only of technique but of 'slow modesty'.[12]

Still, and at the same time as he followed the required model of mastering the history of philosophy, Deleuze also ended up telling that history differently. Even in this early work, his is a project neither of exegesis nor application. Rather, his aim is to think through/with/against these philosophers and to create something new through these encounters. And although his oeuvre may at first seem to be characterized by 'a rather bewildering eclecticism', we can, in fact, discern two strategies of dealing with the tradition of philosophy.[13] To begin with, he focuses on authors who in different ways challenge the rationalist tradition of this history. Thus Daniel W. Smith notes how Deleuze's decision to publish his first book on Hume was a provocation. In an era increasingly dominated by phenomenology, to write on empiricism was evidence of 'the heterodox tendencies of his thought'.[14] Other philosophers, such as Spinoza and Nietzsche, also become central to Deleuze's development of his own philosophy, because they share a critique of the emphasis on interiority that characterized much contemporary thought. Deleuze's second strategy is to approach the history of philosophy as 'a sort of buggery'. This formulation, which we can see the beginnings of in the epigraph to this chapter, and which certainly seems to speak against the idea of humility in relation to one's predecessors, continues: 'It was really important for it to be his own child, because the author had to actually say all I had him saying. But the child was bound to be monstrous too, because it resulted from all sorts of shifting, slipping, dislocations, and hidden emissions.'[15]

This strategy may come across as provocative – and indeed, there were those who saw this work on other authors as a betrayal.[16] Others saw it as true inventiveness. Serres, for example, argues that Deleuze's disengagement from the traditional history of philosophy constituted 'an excellent example of the dynamic movement of a free and inventive thought'.[17] But regardless of how it was perceived, it is safe to say that Deleuze's way of working constituted a rather unusual way of dealing with the history of philosophy. He rejected the idea of simply writing about or 'reflecting on' things, as it keeps philosophy in a passive and non-creative mode incapable of movement. 'What we should in fact do, is stop allowing philosophers to reflect "on" things. The philosopher creates, he doesn't reflect.'[18] This is important to keep in mind when reading Deleuze's early books. They should not be seen as books aiming to account for and explain a philosopher or philosophy but must be seen as a 'thinking with' – a project of picking up and speaking with and through earlier philosophers. As Schrift points out with reference to Deleuze's Nietzsche book, it 'is not titled *Nietzsche's Philosophy* but *Nietzsche "and" Philosophy*', and it not only provides us with an interpretation of Nietzsche, but it provides Deleuze with some crucial components to be developed in his own philosophy.[19] Another way of putting it is to think of the 'in between'. For Deleuze, thinking occurs as an event, one that we cannot hope to, and should not aim to, be able to ascribe to a single locus. It is made possible by nomadism and becomings, 'capture and thefts, interregnums'.[20] In other words, true thinking can occur only when we abandon our ambition of doing it alone. As we will see when we arrive at Deleuze and his friendships later on, when real creation or thinking occurs, 'you're always working in a group, even when you seem to be on your own.'[21]

The monstrous child that is Deleuze's philosophy, then, is such because it does not position Deleuze or the philosopher he writes on as separate and clearly delineated subjects in communication, but rather strives to occur through the shifting and slipping that is initiated when habitual thoughts are disrupted. This, as we will see further in the Conclusion, is a strategy that Deleuze in no way reserved for himself but recommended also to those tempted to write 'on' him once he himself had become more established. This approach is further illuminated when, later on, Deleuze borrows Foucault's words to describe the process of writing his book on him: 'I wanted to find Foucault's double, in the sense he gave the word: "a repetition, another layer, the return of the same, a catching on something else, an imperceptible difference, a coming apart and ineluctable tearing open."'[22] What becomes apparent here, and what becomes apparent also if you are acquainted with Deleuze's philosophical works, is the centrality of difference as an effect of repetition. Indeed, his major work *Difference and Repetition*, which is the principal thesis of his *doctorat d'État* in 1969 (both this and his secondary thesis, *Spinoza et le problème de l'expression* [*Expressionism in Philosophy: Spinoza*, 1990], were published in 1968[23]), focuses, as the title suggests, on establishing this relation.

However, Deleuze's interest in difference in itself, that is, difference that does not depend on identity and contradiction, emerged well before he wrote his doctoral dissertation. He had already worked through this relation in his earlier research, as Bianco notes, inspired by while also questioning his teacher Hyppolite's reliance on Hegel, and proposing instead Bergson as a philosopher of difference without negation.[24] This is outlined in a presentation he made at the Société des amis de Bergson in 1954, published two years later as 'La Conception de la différence chez Bergson'.[25] And indeed, a critical starting point for this rethinking of difference and repetition, which was to become essential to Deleuze's conception of ontology throughout the rest of his work, is what he himself calls an 'anti-Hegelianism'. This takes the shape of a firm resistance to the way the primacy of identity positions negativity as its opposite, and difference as an outcome that is predicated only in relation to such synthesis. In such a configuration, and indeed in much of the history of philosophy, difference and repetition are subordinated to identity in a 'regime of representation'. Deleuze's project is to free difference and repetition from this bind, as he not only finds it incorrect in a modern world characterized by a letting go of beliefs in identity, sameness and transcendent truths, but finds that it serves to prevent real thinking. 'Difference is not and cannot be thought in itself, so long as it is subject to the requirements of representation.'[26] Liberated from the 'tyranny of the same' that is representation, however, difference can be perceived not in relation to identity, but in and of itself. At the same time, the movement of repetition is revealed to generate difference quite apart from the supposed sameness that it repeats. In other words, the movements of difference and repetition are not bound to some transcendent principle but occur immanently. Immanence, a key and defining notion in Deleuze's philosophy, emerges from a conception of ontology without transcendence, that is, without a notion of meaning, truth, or subject or God as somehow standing above and determining existence. Rather, Deleuze sees how more or less stable forms – what Deleuze and Guattari call 'strata' – emerge from a fundamental flow of difference, or chaos. These strata are not different from their surroundings in kind but appear as forms because in them, the flow of difference is slowed down. Some strata are more stable than others but essentially they are still defined in terms of a reduction of difference. In the constant play between difference and repetition, the latter takes over. This is how we come to perceive identity.

Our daily lives are characterized by the 'common sense' of representation and identity – we need 'the habit of saying I' in order to function in an everyday sense. But there is also a danger in this habit: we do not truly see, create or think while relying on it. Philosophically, this common sense keeps thought within pre-determined routes. Politically, the consequences are dangerous and potentially devastating as we are susceptible to being interpellated by institutions and political systems that eliminate difference, determining which attributes are allowed to return in order to shape our identities. This is why creative activity has political significance to the extent that it challenges habitual formations. The problem that such activity encounters, however, while also being part of its potential, is that it 'isn't very compatible with circuits of information and communication, readymade circuits that are compromised from the outset'.[27] What creative activity does, whether by means of philosophy or art or writing or cinema, is that it affirms another kind of repetition. This is a repetition that recognizes and affirms the difference underlying all being (which, then, is not really being, but becoming). This is a more chaotic and creative repetition that does not return to the same but disrupts the habitual by confirming difference. This repetition is a challenge that engenders thought, engenders creativity, engenders becoming. A major reason why Deleuze finds art and literature so central to his thinking is that while they, of course, can also rely on habit, as does much mainstream culture, they also harbour the potential to disrupt habit – they make us see, think, feel in unexpected ways. 'Each art', he writes, 'has its interrelated techniques or repetitions, the critical and revolutionary power of which may attain the highest degree and lead us from the sad repetitions of habit to the profound repetitions of memory.'[28] This disruption of habit that happens when working 'in between' philosophy and art also constitutes a crucial explanation to Deleuze's strategy more generally, working 'in between' himself and previous philosophers (as outlined here) and also between friends.

With this philosophy of difference in mind, we can return to the importance of recognizing Deleuze's strategy of 'thinking with' when reading his early books, and modify and extend it to his oeuvre as a whole. Even if he never came back to writing books thinking through other philosophers in the same overt and methodical way as he did in this early period (with the exception of his book on Foucault in 1986 and on Leibniz in 1988), he continued working with, or 'in between', thinkers throughout his life. There is, of course, his work with Guattari and his dialogues with Parnet, but we also need to note that in books that have no other name than his on the cover, Deleuze always worked through what he at one point called 'mediators'. Creation and true thinking, he argues, are impossible without them: 'They can be people', he suggests, 'but things too, even plants or animals', and 'whether they're real or imaginary, animate or inanimate, you have to form your mediators' because without them, you do not get anywhere – 'you're lost'.[29]

But it took a while for Deleuze to find his mediators and for the groups enabling his own thinking to fully emerge. After the first book, on Hume, it took almost a decade before his second book, *Nietzsche et la philosophie* (*Nietzsche and Philosophy*, 1983), was published in 1962. Deleuze describes this as a period of latency, but not necessarily an unproductive one. On the one hand, he describes it as a hole in his life, as 'catalepsies, or a kind of sleepwalking through a number of years', but on the other, he suggests that it may be in such holes and gaps that movement really happens. Maybe you get beyond the point where you are banging your head against the wall not by escaping but by staying put.[30] But if this period between the early 1950s and 1960s was one of remaining still in some ways, in other ways it was not. In 1956, Deleuze met and married Denise Paul Grandjouan – 'Fanny' – who came to be his partner for life. They had Julien, their first child, in 1960 and their second, Émilie, in 1964. With Fanny came also a house in Saint-Léonard-de-Noblat in Limousin, a house and a region that came to matter very much to Deleuze and where he and the family ended up spending several months every summer.

Not only are these, of course, large events in terms of Deleuze's personal life, but they came to influence his thinking. Fanny's ideas, he describes, 'always seized me from behind, coming from far away in another direction, so that we crossed all the more like the signals from two lamps'.[31] I would like to take pause and note how this idea of approaching someone from behind appears here in what is a less than common way of describing a heterosexual marriage. If we find it remarkable that Deleuze, who was more than once suspected of having homosexual leanings, does not hesitate to describe his encounter with earlier, and exclusively male, philosophers in this manner, it seems even more extraordinary that he is also happy to describe his encounters with his wife in this same way. Fanny, who was a translator of D. H. Lawrence into French, influenced Deleuze's thinking in many different ways. Although her name

The garden surrounding Fanny and Gilles' house in Saint-Léonard-de-Noblat, Limousin.

seems to have fallen away when it was republished, she was also credited as Deleuze's co-writer in the original publication of the essay 'Nietzsche and Saint Paul, Lawrence and John of Patmos' as a preface to D. H. Lawrence's novel *Apocalypse* (1978).[32] Deleuze also repeatedly refers to her not just as a domestic partner, but as a co-thinker: 'Fanny imagines . . .', 'According to Fanny . . .', 'Homage to Fanny . . .'.[33]

Fanny also played an important role in the exchange of writings between Deleuze and Guattari, frequently acting as an intermediary between the two. Their letters and texts in progress often passed through her, and she took an active part in commenting on them. Diary entries by and letters from Guattari reveal her impact on their joint writing as well as his own thinking:

It's true that she is implicated – by symmetry – in this whole thing. But instead of trying to redo it, I became engulfed in narcissistic annihilation: it's worthless, it's shit, 'personological'

soup . . . She sort of hinted at this by telling me that after
Ginsberg, whose book was lying on the table, it's hard to find
a mode of expression.[34]

Indeed, Deleuze gives Fanny credit for the very central notion
of the 'pick-up' as a way of describing the procedure of working
with and through the thinking of others. This is 'the double theft,
the a-parallel evolution' that 'does not happen between persons,
it happens between ideas, each one being deterritorialized in
the other, following a line or lines which are neither in one nor
the other'.[35]

When pushed to defend his seemingly 'conventional' family life
in a period when many, including himself, questioned bourgeois
constructions and conventions of family, Deleuze admits that
'Non-oedipal love is pretty hard work', but he also says that avoiding
the Oedipal is not as simple as to 'be unmarried, not to have kids,
to be gay, to belong to this or that group'. The only way of fighting
the Oedipal is 'by fighting yourself, by experimenting on yourself,
by opening yourself up to love and desire'.[36] The dynamics between
him and Fanny and Guattari were clearly very productive but not
uncomplicated in this very respect. Guattari's diary entries reveal
that he harboured love and desire for both Deleuze and Fanny and
that he struggled to keep free from Oedipal inscription.[37] We will
return to the notions of love and desire later, but for now, we can
note that Fanny was part of Deleuze's 'thinking with': 'the AND
Felix, AND Fanny, AND you, AND all those of whom we speak, AND
me'. She appears, with the others, 'as so many distorted images in
running water'.[38]

Looking at the articles, essays and reviews later collected in
the volume *L'Île déserte et autres textes: textes et entretiens, 1953–1974*
(2002; *Desert Islands and Other Texts, 1953–1974*, 2003), we can see
that Deleuze was not completely out of the academic loop during
these years. In the 1950s, he read and worked through Nietzsche's

texts. Nietzsche had, as Schrift notes, surfaced on the reading list for the *agrégation de philosophie* in 1958, making this the first time that he was picked up by professional philosophers in France. *On the Genealogy of Morality* was on this list in 1958–9, when Deleuze was starting his university career teaching at the Sorbonne, and he taught the book in autumn 1958 – which, as Schrift suggests, may explain the centrality of this book in *Nietzsche and Philosophy*.[39] Wahl's lectures on Nietzsche towards the end of this decade also helped Deleuze prepare for this 1962 monograph. During the latter part of the decade, he also wrote the aforementioned essay on Bergson (in 1956) and edited a collection of his texts in 1957.[40] During this period he held a number of different teaching positions at different lycées and universities – at Amiens, Orléans and Louis-le-Grand high school in Paris, and from 1957 he became a highly appreciated assistant professor at the Sorbonne. Finding teaching an important part of his life, he also spent much time preparing courses. Although at a later stage, and increasingly marked by illness, he found that it took more energy than it gave and was glad, eventually, to give it up, Deleuze found teaching inspirational and worthwhile for many of his thirty years as a university professor. Students interviewed by Dosse recall how Deleuze's sessions on Wednesday afternoons were packed to the point where some had to stand in the corridor, with the door left open so they could hear. Deleuze, who was a very young professor for such an esteemed institution, is described to have delivered spellbinding seminars and 'answers for everything', often combined with unexpected twists and directions.[41] Alain Badiou, who was a student at the École normale supérieure at the time, and who later became Deleuze's colleague at Université Paris-VIII at Vincennes, recalls hearing rumours of Deleuze's 'extraordinary lectures' accompanied by his 'astonishing corporeal presence' and which, 'ranging from Hume to *La Nouvelle Héloïse*, were singularly different from everything that was recited elsewhere'.[42]

During the first years of the 1960s, Deleuze had a research appointment at the CNRS (Centre national de la recherche scientifique). While on this break from teaching, Deleuze began to read philosophy and literature beyond his teaching and he published a first study on Leopold von Sacher-Masoch, 'De Sacher-Masoch au masochisme', in 1961. With this followed by the publication of *Nietzsche and Philosophy* in 1962, the supposed dry spell was over. And soon followed his books on Kant in 1963, Bergson in 1966, Sacher-Masoch in 1967 and Spinoza in 1968. If we put together his period of intense teaching and the writing of these early books, this part of Deleuze's life emerges as a trajectory of his coming into being as a philosopher, both as a person and as a thinker. His later work becomes much easier to understand if read through these earlier studies. As Michael Hardt notes, the 'subterranean research' that Deleuze conducted during this period followed a decidedly different course than those of most of his contemporaries. And perhaps, Hardt suggests, it is Deleuze's forging of 'new paths, outside the limelight and commonplaces of public French cultural debates' during this formative period that 'allowed him to surface with such a profound impact later'.[43] Deleuze was in some ways out of sync with a contemporary intellectual arena profoundly engaged with Hegel and Heidegger, with Husserl and phenomenology, with Marxist theory, linguistics and, down the line, with deconstruction. Instead, he dug deep into a history of philosophy that was not particularly fashionable. At the same time, Deleuze's coming into being must be understood not so much as a mobilization of a philosopher-identity as the opening up of a philosopher-becoming. How many Deleuzes can we find in his work, asks Véronique Bergen, suggesting that his philosophy 'is diffracted into as many senses as there are forces taking hold of it'.[44]

And new forces were certainly at play in the late 1960s and early 1970s. Having taught at the Sorbonne from 1957 to 1960, been on a release from the Sorbonne to work at the CNRS between 1960 and

1964, and after that taught at the University of Lyon from 1964 to 1969, Deleuze defended his major doctoral thesis at the Sorbonne in early 1969. At this point of course he had already written several books (a fact that he himself suggests can be explained by the common reaction of not wanting to finish your thesis) and he recalls that the event itself was a rather awkward one. Parnet jokingly suggests during one of their dialogues that one reason for this awkwardness might have been that at this point he was already better known than the people on the committee. This is not quite true, however, and Deleuze explains the discomfort as stemming rather from the anxieties of the committee regarding the security of the event. Deleuze's was one of the first doctoral defences after the May '68 events and the committee feared that gangs of students would try to interfere with it. Deleuze recalls that a lot of effort was put into finding the safest location for the event, and adds somewhat jokingly that the committee did not pay as much attention to him as they did to watching the door for potential intruders.[45] And he seems to have recognized, not without pleasure, the changes in the air. In a letter to Clément Rosset dated 7 May 1968, he mentions that he would like to see his masters at the university in Paris, but adds, with a touch of irony, the qualification '(if they have not been eaten by then).'[46]

Indeed, Deleuze was very positively inclined towards the student upheavals. He publicly supported the protests and attended many of the events during these turbulent months. He was frequently seen on the streets with students and also joined, for example, the occupation of a room at a radio station, to which he helped gain access via a former student. His supervisor, Maurice de Gandillac, once arrived at Deleuze's house to discover that his children, Julien and Émilie, had hung red flags and posters from the balcony.[47] However, Deleuze was never a revolutionary in the way Guattari and many of his contemporaries were, and unlike many of his friends he never joined the French Communist Party. He says that this was not so much due to a lack of sympathy (he had, since 1945, identified as a 'homme de gauche' – a leftist) as it was to a lack of time, a personal reluctance towards groups and talking to strangers, and also a wavering belief in some of the strategies involved. It would have been more efficient, he argues, for people to finish their dissertations than to collect signatures for petitions. Being a leftist, for Deleuze, is a matter of perception. It is about 'perceiving the horizon' and about recognizing that becomings occur through minorities. Revolutions, however, are doomed to fail or to go bad eventually. It is nonsense to think otherwise. But this does not mean that we should not encourage them: that we should not affirm a becoming-revolutionary in an intolerable world.[48] Deleuze is positive towards May '68 exactly as such an event and, being thrown 'into the stew' of the subsequent turmoil by Guattari,[49] they together came to be seen as pathfinders of the time.

The year 1969 also came with a permanent teaching position at the experimental Université Paris-VIII in Vincennes (later moved to its current location at Saint-Denis in 1980). Eager to return to Paris, Deleuze tried to reintroduce himself at the Sorbonne but found the exercise disastrous. As he describes it in a letter to Klossowski, it felt like the experience of the good boy who thinks he is loved but discovers he is hated. 'This is a serious blow to my pride.'[50] The University of Paris VIII, however, ended up suiting him much better. It had only just been founded (first as the Centre universitaire expérimental de Vincennes and from 1971 as a university proper), and Foucault had been invited to establish its philosophy department; Deleuze was one of the first he invited to join that department. Eventually, it also came to harbour not only Deleuze but many other central thinkers of the time, such as Châtelet, Lyotard, Serres and Jacques Lacan, as well as thinkers who would soon become central, including Hélène Cixous, Alain Badiou, Étienne Balibar and Rancière. Born in the wake of the political and intellectual turmoil of 1968, the explicit intention for its founding

University of Paris VIII in Saint-Denis.

was to respond to student calls for a modernized university and more intellectual freedom. Compared with the earlier job at Lyon, of which he had not been too fond, this environment was a more suitable match for Deleuze, who was inspired by the educational and ethical diversity of his students' backgrounds as well as by their broad range of interests and abilities.[51] This was the beginning of a new and highly productive period of Deleuze's life. At Paris VIII, he was to give weekly seminars until he retired in 1987. Students had to come early to secure a seat at these highly appreciated seminars where, Hugh Tomlinson and Barbara Habberjam note, the tiny room was packed with smoke and the discussions ranged 'from Spinoza to modern music, from Chinese metallurgy to bird-song, from linguistics to gang warfare'.[52]

Much as this intellectual and vigorous milieu suited him, the philosophy department where he taught was also shaken by a number of internal conflicts during the 1970s. University strikes supported by the department, disagreements between this department and others, and decisions not to renew some of the numerous part-time teaching contracts in place, which were seen as a controversial coup to get rid of unwanted elements, created large rifts within the philosophy department and darkened its reputation. The experimental and nonconventional practices of the faculty members also placed them under severe critique from the government. Deleuze was involved in many of these concerns and conflicts in various ways. His position during these 'red years', as Badiou calls them, was also somewhat controversial. Maoists such as Badiou see Deleuze and the 'anarcho-desirers' he inspired as 'an enemy all the more formidable for being internal to the "movement"'.[53] Badiou recalls attacking Deleuze 'with the heavy verbal artillery of the epoch', writing enraged articles and even, at one point, commanding a 'brigade' to intervene in one of Deleuze's courses. Under attack particularly was Deleuze's conception of the relation between politics and mass movements. Deleuze, Badiou recalls, remained calm, almost paternal, throughout these assaults, only once picking up the fight when he thought Badiou was part of a group taking over the department for political ends. At one

One of Deleuze's seminars at Vincennes.

point during these stormy times, Deleuze created a 'Polytechnic Institute of Philosophy' with his friend and colleague Châtelet (who was also the chair of the department, following the departure of Foucault to the Collège de France), to encourage students to remain in the department and to pursue degrees writing on one of the arts that would also give them a diploma recognized by future employers.[54] While the institute worked, Deleuze's good friend and colleague Réne Schérer suggests in an interview that Deleuze had undoubtedly overestimated his students' creative potential.[55] This was a turbulent period, in other words, in a turbulent space but with people eager to think afresh – with all the challenges that such energy generates.

And it was not all conflict. Many connections with contemporary colleagues and philosophers were initiated or intensified during this period and many of these would also become political collaborators during what was to be a period of political involvement for Deleuze stretching across the 1970s. He worked closely with Châtelet at Paris VIII, and Foucault, whom he had already known for a while, became an important collaborator in the activism of the period. At this time, Deleuze and his work also had many points of connection with Lyotard and the latter's writing on libidinal economies. Importantly, 1969 also saw the beginning of Deleuze's productive friendship with Guattari. In 1972 they published their first major collaborative work, *L'Anti-Œdipe* (*Anti-Oedipus: Capitalism and Schizophrenia*, 1977), which, along with the second volume *A Thousand Plateaus* in 1980, has been seen as consolidating and expressing the political events of 1968. Friendship and politics, as we shall see presently, would be part of many productive encounters over the coming decades.

3
A Friendship

I stole Félix, and I hope he did the same for me.[1]

Deleuze had a very rich understanding of friendship and this is
mirrored in the many different kinds of friendship he developed
through his life. We have already mentioned a few, like the
formative meeting with Halbwachs in his youth and his long
friendship with Tournier. Other contemporaries, like Badiou, give
witness to a sort of 'nonrelationship', in their case a series of fraught
disagreements over philosophy as well as politics that nonetheless
resulted in an exchange of letters lasting for years.[2] Exchanging
reflections and ideas with close as well as more distant friends was
central to Deleuze's mode of thinking – of thinking with. Thus we
see, for example, how an exchange of letters with the contemporary
French philosopher and writer Clément Rosset stretched over
decades. This exchange stimulated ponderings about the need for
new forms of philosophy in the mid-1960s, evinced an excitement
over mutual interest in Nietzsche, and inspired the idea of the
refrain in the 1980s. The letters reveal Deleuze's excitement over
the ideas sparked by Rosset – one letter is full of questions posed
one after another and a near impatient request for further input:
'when you have the time, can you give me further guidance here?'[3]
Lettres et autres textes, a collection of Deleuze's letters published in
2015, demonstrates how he was exchanging letters also with other
philosophers, poets, editors, political intellectuals and students

such as Alain Vinson, Châtelet, Jean Piel, Klossowki, Foucault, Gherasim Luca, Arnaud Villani, Joseph Emmanuel Voeffray, Elias Sanbar, Jean-Clet Martin, André Bernold and, of course, Guattari.

Deleuze's understanding of friendship is not 'that of a common and ideal bond and can hardly be encapsulated in a neat definition' – if, indeed, such neat definition of friendship is ever possible.[4] As Charles J. Stivale outlines in a book devoted to the many prisms of Deleuze and friendship, friendship is a central aspect of Deleuze's work in many different ways – friendship is about pedagogy, it is about thought, it is about the encounter, it is about the comical, the impersonal, the dialogic, about love and distance, about joy and about experimentation.[5] Friendship, Deleuze says in *L'Abécédaire*, is about perception. He also uses the notion of charm to describe the basic attraction of friendship – a charm that is impersonal, a charm that is the hum of intensities, affects, moods and sensations. Before we even have time to formulate specific thoughts or opinions about a person, we may perceive a gesture, an opening, an awakening that goes to the very root of perception, and this, he explains to Parnet, constitutes a friendship. The charm of a friend is also associated with some degree of madness: 'If you can't grasp the small trace of madness in someone, you can't be their friend.'[6] It is, if we were to begin to try to find one thing that brings all Deleuze's rich ways of understanding and practising friendship together, about vibrations – that hum that is creative; it creates love, it creates thinking and it creates writing.

But for Deleuze, friendship is also necessarily about friction, about being out of sync. Just as he calls for a critique of philosophy, a critique of friendship is necessary to the extent that both philosophy and friendship tend to rely on a mutual goodwill – a communication of the conventional, a reliance on the possible. Such philosophy and such friendship remain 'ignorant of the dark regions in which are elaborated the effective forces that act on thought, the determinations that *force* us to think.'[7] To get to true thinking, a philosophical friendship needs to affirm its dark regions. The friction of uneven surfaces and the ensuing sparks are what cause the creative hum. There needs to be joy but also a kind of productive distrust. As Deleuze writes in a letter to Dionys Mascolo, a friend to whom, Stivale notes, he is partly indebted when it comes to developing his understanding of friendship: 'One would go that far, to wariness of a friend, and all of that would, with friendship, put the "distress" in thought in an essential way.'[8] This distress seems to develop in his thinking from something negative to something positive. While an early Deleuze suggests that friendship is about false communications and misunderstandings – that 'only art gives us what we vainly sought from a friend' – Stivale notes how a Deleuze who has worked with Guattari seems to have discovered the necessity of the friend for thinking.[9] Distress becomes important because it resists the sedimentation of thinking and being. True friendship is not about two individuals in an established relation to each other but about pulling each other out of the self. 'Stealing Félix' and expecting to be stolen back, as the epigraph above begins to suggest, means insisting that Deleuze and Guattari's work is not the result of two authors working together so much as the outcome of working 'between the two'.

We can better understand what this 'between the two' means for Deleuze and how it informed his practices both philosophically and personally – if those two are indeed separable for him – if we also understand the concept of the fold. The fold, a concept that Deleuze associates with the Baroque and the philosophy of Leibniz, and which he discusses at length in *Le Pli: Leibniz et le baroque* (1988; *The Fold: Leibniz and the Baroque*, 1993), is essentially about moving away from conceptions of inside and outside. Like Baroque architecture that curves and folds and twists and in which it is often hard to determine where the inside might end and the outside begin, Deleuze sees the fold as a means of rethinking ideas of the self as somehow existing separately from its surroundings. The fold shows how the subject does not transcend its environment; it does not pre-exist the point of view, the thought or the affect, but rather it is momentarily created through them: 'a subject will be what comes to the point of view, or rather what remains in the point of view.'[10] What is produced this way is not a subject but an individuation effect. Thinking in terms of individuation means recognizing that seeing, thinking and feeling cannot be ascribed to an individual subject but happen through encounters that generate such effects. Through these conceptions of the fold and individuation we can begin to see how absolutely essential friendship is for Deleuze on every level. Indeed, friendship, understood as a joint becoming, is a precondition for philosophy. This is underlined by the way Deleuze and Guattari link friendship back to the ancient Greeks. The Greeks 'force' the friend into a relationship that is not a convivial one between two competent entities. The friend 'who appears in philosophy no longer stands for an extrinsic persona, an example or empirical circumstance, but rather for a presence that is intrinsic to thought, a condition of possibility of thought itself'.[11]

Deleuze's many letters and exchanges with friends about philosophy reflect this notion of friendship as a condition for philosophy. Among them, his friendship with Guattari stands out and shines with particular intensity. Once asked if there was an emerging rhizome formed by Deleuze-Guattari-Foucault-Lyotard-Klossowski, Deleuze responded that such a rhizome could have happened, but it did not: 'There is only a rhizome between Felix and me.'[12] Deleuze and Guattari's friendship started with an exchange of letters in 1969. Guattari sought out Deleuze but it was Deleuze who initiated their collaboration. These first exchanges seem to have emerged from a mutual curiosity. Already in this early exchange, Deleuze identifies key elements of interest in Guattari's work – the notion of the schizo, for example, and of transversality. He also encourages Guattari in an effort to help him get over his writer's block. He advises him not to wait until the work feels perfect: publish it anyway – you can always come back to it later! Writing is a way of feeling better, he writes, of getting yourself out of the furnace.[13]

Deleuze seems greatly inspired and enthusiastic in these early letters. He wants to develop Guattari's ideas about non-Oedipal sexuality and transversality, he finds Guattari's responses beautiful and rigorous, and he poses series of questions that, he hopes, Guattari will have the inspiration to answer (preferably in an orderly fashion).[14] Most centrally, Deleuze is attracted to Guattari's ambition of developing psychoanalysis beyond the framework of his former teacher, Jacques Lacan. He finds this ambition extremely rich and in need of further theorization. For those interested in the emergence of Deleuze and Guattari's collaboration, Deleuze's letters published in *Lettres et autres textes* and Guattari's diary entries and letters to Deleuze collected in *The Anti-Oedipus Papers* provide a rich account of how their joint thinking emerged as well as continued through the years. It is intriguing to be allowed insight into the process of development of concepts that later come to be central to their work. 'Could you explain to me with patience,' Deleuze writes to Guattari in 1981, for example, 'why you give apparent privilege to expression [over content] from the point of view of the assemblage?'[15]

Their first joint book, *Anti-Oedipus*, took shape first with the help of 'long, disorderly letters' and then by meeting 'for several days or weeks at the time', just the two of them. During these meetings,

we didn't dialogue: one of us would speak, and the other would listen. I refused to let Félix go, even when he had had enough, and Félix kept after me, even when I was exhausted. Gradually, a concept would acquire an autonomous existence.[16]

In this process, Deleuze saw Guattari as the diamond miner and himself as the polisher.[17] 'You are a formidable inventor of raw concepts,' he writes to Guattari, and insists that these concepts do emerge from him – not from external causes, as Guattari himself seems to think.[18] Describing their collaboration, they both insist on getting away from the focus on them as two separate and knowledgeable subjects performing a purely intellectual exchange. 'This collaboration', Guattari writes,

> is not the result of a simple meeting between two people. In addition to the particular circumstances leading up to it, there was also a political context. At the outset, it was less a matter of sharing a common understanding than sharing the sum of our uncertainties and even a certain discomfort and confusion with respect to the way that May 1968 had turned out.

Deleuze describes their process as one of trying to break with duality:

> we tried to get beyond this traditional duality because two of us were writing. Neither of us was the patient, nor the psychiatrist, but we had to be both to establish a process . . . That process is what we called the flux.[19]

Deleuze and Guattari wanted to see themselves as a machinic assemblage from which collective utterances emerge. This is something that Deleuze came to argue more generally: 'There is no expressing subject, i.e. subject of utterance, but only assemblages.'[20] While naming some of his collaborators, he stresses that these 'points – Félix, Claire Parnet, myself and many others – did not count and only served as temporary, transitory, fleeting points of subjectivation.'[21] Trying to determine who wrote what would be to work against this very idea and to establish subject positions where they were not sought.

The process was not always easy, however, and after the completion of the manuscript for *Anti-Oedipus*, which was to be published in 1972, Guattari expressed a discomforting loss of self that he did not seem to appreciate. Unable to write and unable not to write, he struggled with a feeling that 'the ship is going down'.[22] This seemed to stem from an acute awareness of the differences between him and Deleuze – 'We're really not of the same dimension' – and from a feeling of his own insufficiency in the face of Deleuze's focus and ambition. Here we get a sense, then, that while their differences proved productive, some – for example what Guattari describes as Deleuze's productivity and always having 'the *oeuvre* in mind', and Guattari's own more chaotic 'fucking-around-o-maniacal schizo flow' – also generated a '"distress" in thought' that was quite painful. Feeling 'a bit overcoded by *Anti-Oedipus*', by the way his raw material had taken a more consistent shape, Guattari was anxious about standing accountable for *Anti-Oedipus* after its pending publication: 'What I feel like is just fucking around. Publish this diary for example. Say stupid shit.'[23]

The process of finding a way back to the productive dimensions of letting go of the self took a path via Franz Kafka.[24] Deleuze and Guattari's joint book *Kafka: Pour une littérature mineure* (*Kafka: Toward a Minor Literature*, 1986) was published in 1975, that is, between the two *Capitalism and Schizophrenia* books. This study offers the theories of folding, individuation and assemblage that would come to guide Deleuze and Guattari's joint philosophy from then on, not the least in *A Thousand Plateaus*, the second *Capitalism and Schizophrenia* book, published in 1980. By the time they wrote this third book together, the experience and process of writing had changed:

> Félix and I had developed such a good working relationship that the one could guess where the other was headed. Our conversations now were full of ellipses, and we were able to establish various resonances, not between us, but among the various disciplines that we were traversing.[25]

Deleuze and Guattari.

After the intense collaborations of these first years of friendship,
Deleuze went on to pursue a kind of friendship with art, literature
and philosophy in the 1980s – 'a specific practice of friendship', as
Stivale puts it, 'an intimate exchange through which these modes
of creation elicit a production of thought'[26] – while Guattari went
on to pursue his radical political engagements. We 'each had to
return to our own work, so we could catch our breath', as Deleuze
puts it, but he also felt 'certain that we will work together again'.[27]
And indeed they did resume their collaboration, trying to answer
a question that Deleuze had brought up in a letter to Guattari in
1981: 'At the centre for me would be to search for a clear and simple
answer to the question: what is philosophy?'[28] Their fourth and final
book together, published in 1991, was *Qu'est-ce que la philosophie?*
(*What is Philosophy?*, 1994). It is sometimes suggested that Deleuze
wrote this book almost entirely by himself and included Guattari
as a co-author as something of a gift to his ill and dying friend.
Whether or not this is true, the very notion tells us something about

the entanglements of friendship and philosophy that characterized the relationship between Deleuze and Guattari.

Throughout the years from 1969 until Guattari's death in 1992, Deleuze and Guattari developed a friendship that is not entirely easy to define. It becomes clear from their early exchange of letters that they were attracted to each other's thinking, and also that they seemed to sense the richness and atemporal quality of their emerging friendship from the very beginning. Guattari writes that their pending first meeting will be 'an event with several origins that is already retroactively present'.[29] 'I too', Deleuze writes, 'feel that we have become friends before having actually met.'[30] Dosse's account of their friendship is somewhat inconsistent, and maybe that is what it was. On the one hand, he suggests, they were never to be very close, and on the other he provides accounts of their friendship as intensely loving and trusting.[31] This can also be seen in their letters. Both writers, despite being quite comfortable using the more informal *tu* when addressing others, continued addressing each other with the formal *vous*. At the same time, we see closeness as well as a loving tenderness: 'Je vous embrasse fort.'[32]

I would like to suggest two strategies for understanding this seeming contradiction. To begin with, we may want to question what we read into the idea of closeness. Deleuze and Guattari did keep a certain distance. However, this is a distance that predicates closeness of a more intricate and perhaps intimate kind, one that is less between persons and more between singularities: 'There is a real politics of dissent between us,' Guattari explains, 'not so much a cult as a culture of heterogeneity, such that each recognizes and accepts the other's singularity . . . Gilles is my friend, not my buddy.'[33] And indeed, and with the understanding of friendship that I have begun to sketch above, I would suggest that the trope of stealing and being stolen outlined in the epigraph to this chapter suggests a most acute intimacy, albeit on a less conventional plane. To let go of ideas of fixed borders of self and other while also avoiding polarization is to enter into a process of becoming-imperceptible, to open life to productive encounters. Deleuze, who seems not to have been too interested in conventional relations, describes a very particular kind of intimacy when he suggests that he wants 'just to have imperceptible relationships with imperceptible people, that's what is most beautiful in the world. You can say that we are all molecules, a molecular network.'[34]

Not only friendship but love too needs to be rethought under such circumstances. Love is not an obvious notion when dealing with Deleuze, largely because we tend to associate love with certain recognizable structures and individuals. 'Love is a Cogito built for two,' write Deleuze and Guattari in *A Thousand Plateaus*, and this is not the kind of process that would take us anywhere Deleuze would want to take us. Indeed, the triangular process of writing that involved not only Deleuze and Guattari but Fanny, as outlined earlier, speaks to love, desire and thinking beyond the cogito. 'No reason', Guattari writes in his diary, 'to set desire *for* Fanny in opposition to desire *for* Gilles.'[35] Love that strengthens the molar – built on possessiveness, jealousy, the economy of individuals – does not have the power to fuel becomings. And still, Deleuze mentions the notion of love recurrently. In the Introduction, I mentioned love as a recognition of singularities, multiplicities and 'little events', and in the previous chapter I mentioned it again in relation to non-Oedipal love. This would also be the love Deleuze seems to have felt for Guattari: 'the way we understood and complemented, depersonalized and singularized – in short, loved – one another.'[36] This is not a love between egos but a creative, molecular love that creates a sense of productive depersonalization. Clearly bothered by the way readers have tried to ascertain who wrote what in their joint books, Deleuze explains that 'since each of us, like anyone else, is already various people, it gets rather crowded.'[37]

If the first strategy of trying to comprehend Deleuze and Guattari's friendship is to challenge preconceptions about what 'closeness' means, the second is to think about the possibility that their theories about becoming and individuation are actually reflected in their lives and – centrally here – their life together. As Stivale points out, Deleuze describes friends such as Guattari and Foucault by means of the impersonal: through gestures and atmospheres.[38] Deleuze and Guattari's very special combination of work and friendship should not really be explained as a combination at all but rather as a merging, a co-emergence by thinking together, an assemblage. This assemblage can also be seen in the way Deleuze repeatedly describes Guattari not so much as a person but as a series of movements and gestures. Guattari seems to have provided energy and speed when Deleuze was overtaken by the exhaustion that he often describes in their letters: 'Your notes are extremely beautiful', he states, 'while I am slower than ever.'[39] Félix, he writes, was like the sea, 'sparkling with light'; he 'has extraordinary speeds' and 'never *ceases*'.[40] He moved constantly, whether by word, gesture or sound, 'like a kaleidoscope forming a new combination every time'. The name Félix, he suggests, 'denoted something which was happening, and not a subject'.[41] After Guattari's death in 1992, Deleuze wrote:

Perhaps the most painful aspects of remembering a dead friend are the gestures and glances that still reach us, that still come to us long after he is gone. Félix's work gives new substance to these gestures and glances, like a new object capable of transmitting their power.[42]

The gesture returns in Deleuze's description of his friendship with Foucault. 'It's easier', he writes when asked how and when he got to know Foucault, 'to remember a gesture or a laugh than a date.'[43] Deleuze and Foucault met for the first time through a mutual friend in the 1950s but Deleuze himself recalls getting to know Foucault in the early 1960s.[44] This time, their joint interest in Nietzsche brought them together and their first collaboration was on a new

French edition of Nietzsche's work.[45] Their collaborations intensified around 1968, when Deleuze joined the Groupe d'information sur les prisons (GIP), a left-wing activist organization of which Foucault was one of the prime agents. This group, which was intended to spread information about prisons, was part of a larger effort in this period of remodelling the ethics of the intellectual. The aim of this endeavour was to position the intellectual less as someone with universal totalizing claims to knowledge or politics and more as someone directly engaged in 'specific struggles over specific points'.[46] Together, Deleuze and Foucault participated in and organized a number of more or less militant actions in relation to political situations – demonstrations, protests and petitions pertaining not only to prisons but to racism and repression more generally. These actions also involved a number of other intellectuals and writers of the time, including Sartre, Cixous and Jean Genet.[47]

Deleuze and Foucault's friendship was characterized by an intellectual exchange in full awareness that it was largely public. Eleanor Kaufman describes their friendship as informed by a playful but serious innocence, 'one that is joyfully timid in the knowledge that others may be watching'.[48] They also deeply, and often publicly, admired each other's philosophical work. As such, they were not unlike many other twentieth-century intellectuals who, as Kaufman shows, seemed to have a penchant for overtly expressing highly laudatory commentary on each other.[49] Deleuze finds Foucault's mere existence inspiring and admirable. He admires his courage in thought and politics and describes it as 'outlandish', 'shocking' and 'comic' in the best possible way.[50] But in more private conversation too, Deleuze expresses great admiration for Foucault. In comparison with Foucault's oeuvre, which he sees as admirable and novel, he finds his own lacking: it has lots of little nice bits but is compromised by many pieces that are too academic.[51] And he finds Foucault's interpretation of his works quite wonderful: 'I feel that you both fully understand me and surpass me. This is a dream.'[52] Ultimately, Deleuze finds Foucault 'the greatest thinker of our time'.[53]

Foucault, in turn, describes Deleuze as 'the greatest current French philosopher'.[54] Reviewing Deleuze's *Difference and Repetition* and *The Logic of Sense* in 1970, he finds these two books of such exceptional merit 'that they are difficult to discuss'.[55] It is also in this review, which reads a little, Marks notes, 'like a lyrical meditation on Deleuze's thought', that Foucault pronounces the famous, if ambiguous, words: 'perhaps one day, this century will be known as Deleuzian.'[56] Deleuze comments on this remark and on their mutual exchanges in general in his 'Letter to a Harsh Critic', where he rejects the idea that he and Foucault would simply be 'trading compliments. It doesn't seem to cross your mind', he writes, 'that I might really admire Foucault, or that his little remark's a joke meant to make people who like us laugh, and make everyone else livid.'[57] These exchanges also have more nuance to them than the simple trading of compliments. While they were both readily uttering extensive praise for each other, Kaufman notes a distinct imbalance and difference in style in how this is articulated: where Foucault utters more momentary but momentous statements, Deleuze's praise of Foucault comes rather in terms of a 'steady expenditure of Foucault-centered energy'. Ultimately, however, Kaufman admits, it becomes difficult to make this distinction between utterances, since they spoke both with and through each other in an economy in which the boundaries of the two of them as distinct persons were broken.[58]

Still, these boundaries re-emerged with some force in a set of disagreements over politics in the 1970s. Disputes regarding the imprisonment and extradition of the German lawyer Klaus Croissant, who acted as attorney to the Baader-Meinhof gang, and on whether West Germany was a fascist state, as well as a more extended and increasingly divergent analysis of politics put an end to the more active part of Deleuze and Foucault's friendship.[59]

Deleuze, Sartre and Foucault at a GIP action in 1972.

Dosse outlines an additional number of disputes that appeared
over these years. A second point of disagreement between them
regarded the Israel–Palestine conflict, in relation to which Foucault
was considerably more lenient towards Israel than was Deleuze.[60]
Deleuze was strongly affected by the occupation of Palestinian
territory and by the treatment of the Palestinians. In a letter to
Guattari, he expresses a sense of depression and darkness at the
news about the massacres in the refugee camp of Sabra and Shatila
in 1982. 'Everything is dark,' he writes. 'I find what is happening
in Lebanon intolerable.'[61] Deleuze published several texts on the
topic in the late 1970s and early 1980s, such as 'Spoilers of Peace',
'The Indians of Palestine' (an interview with Deleuze's friend the
Palestinian writer and editor Elias Sanbar) and 'The Importance
of Being Arafat', all of which speak to Deleuze's clear stand on
the wrongs of the Israeli occupation of Palestinian territory.[62]
Identifying a core problem in the way the Israeli state is based on
an openly disregarded fact – the Palestinians already living there –
he notes how Palestinians are referred to as 'Palestinian Arabs as if

they were living there by chance or by mistake' and a denial of 'not only the rights but the very fact of Palestinians'.[63]

A third point of disagreement between Deleuze and Foucault was their different views on the *nouveaux philosophes*. This is the name given to a rather disparate group of French philosophers of the 1970s, including among others André Glucksmann, Bernard-Henri Lévy, Pascal Bruckner, Christian Jambet and Guy Lardreau, who, after a flirtation with Maoism as students had in common an affinity for working in unprecedented ways with the media and a rejection of the prevalence of Marxist discourse and of more general leftist tendencies of contemporary as well as older French intellectuals. While Foucault was at least initially more supportive of their ambitions, not the least of their critique of the Gulag, Deleuze proffers heavy criticism of their inclinations more generally. In Deleuze's reaction to these *nouveaux philosophes* we find a good example of his philosophy as expressed in political terms. He was extremely critical of what he saw as their movement towards 'philosophical marketing', their return to the centrality of individual authors, what he saw as their hypocritical political identification with the victims of the Gulag, and their reactive rejection of May '68. The effect of their strategies, he argued in an interview in 1977, is a deadening of thought effected by once again hemming it in to the idea of the individual subject and thus closing down the space for true encounters – encounters that are also essential to the possibility of real political initiative. Their political pessimism as a 'lost generation' after May '68 was in part taken out on Deleuze and Guattari as 'helmsmen' of the '68 generation. Quite apart from the possible personal affront, an explanation Deleuze himself rejects,[64] the pessimism of the *nouveaux philosophes* also stood against Deleuze's refusal of nihilism. Deleuze embraced an affirmative politics even in the midst of dejection, and insisted, as Gregory Flaxman puts it, using Deleuze's own expressions, on the necessity of being worthy of one's own events.[65] Deleuze felt that, in negating politics and experiment, the *nouveaux philosophes* had 'closed the window' where 'once a little breeze was blowing'.[66]

The phenomenon of the *nouveaux philosophes* reinforced the importance of the author in a vein of which both Deleuze and Foucault were highly sceptical. The 'author-function', Deleuze insists, is an empty position, and one that when insisted upon not only encourages the branding and positioning of dead thinking but interferes with active, creative functions that occur necessarily beyond a single subject position. An insistence on the author-function also constitutes a way of hiding the fact that there is little to say – a subject position that takes itself seriously is one that tends to hide its empty propositions. And as he puts it in direct reference to the *nouveaux philosophes*: 'the weaker the thought, the stronger the philosopher.'[67] In other words, insisting on an author-function is a reactive move that hides emptiness at best and obstructs creativity at worst. But at the same time as Deleuze's response to the *nouveaux philosophes* was thus perfectly in line with his philosophical project as a whole, there is also a sense in which we can take the nature of his response as it is articulated as an example of how Deleuze may not always have succeeded in living up to the becoming-active of affirmation. 'My small strength', he writes at one point in a letter to Guattari, 'is never to have answered or participated in any polemic.'[68] But perhaps his response to the *nouveaux philosophes* constitutes an example of where he did not himself quite manage to overcome his own reactive impulses. His one official response to them ('I don't have time to respond more than once. This is it'[69]), Flaxman suggests, is clearly marked by reactive instinct. In his need for condemnation and also, more importantly, for acknowledging and responding to the fact that these philosophers will probably see his rejoinder as a sign of jealousy, there is none of that 'mood of apocalyptic laughter and the creative modalities of "a life"' to which his philosophy aspires.[70]

There were also more purely conceptual disagreements between Deleuze and Foucault. For example, Deleuze was horrified by

Foucault's return to the concept of truth ('Michel is completely nuts'[71]). But perhaps the most central philosophical rift pertained to their differing views on conceptions of desire and pleasure. Deleuze read Foucault's first book on the *History of Sexuality* and found himself having a number of objections. In 1977, Deleuze wrote a letter on the topic to Foucault, which he entrusted Foucault's assistant François Ewald to deliver. Because these notes ended up constituting the last exchange between them, it has been suggested that Foucault was wounded by this letter, to which he did not reply, and that he shortly afterwards decided never to see Deleuze again. The letter came in a period when Foucault was struggling – his book was not very well received and Foucault, Ewald recalls, was going through something of a crisis.[72] And although the letter is not written in a personal or accusatory tone, Deleuze expresses that after reading this book he no longer knows 'how to situate [himself] in terms of Michel's present research'.[73] But Ewald rejects the idea that this letter was articulated as a matter of critique and even less a matter of a polemic. Rather, he suggests, Deleuze wrote the letter because he was sensitive to the hard times that his friend was going through and that it was 'an invitation, entirely imbued with the sincerity of friendship, to take up again a dialogue which had been interrupted.'[74]

In his letter, which was published as 'Désir et plaisir' in 1994 (published in English as 'Desire and Pleasure' in 1997), Deleuze outlines a set of ways in which he and Foucault disagree in their understanding of these concepts. Having in common a denunciation of what they see as the hijacking of sexuality by psychoanalysis, Deleuze and Foucault take very different routes from there. Where Foucault ended up rejecting the usefulness of the concept of desire because of its seemingly inevitable inscription into psychoanalytic discourses and moved on to write his famous three volumes on sexuality with a focus on pleasure, Deleuze rejected, instead, the notion of pleasure as one associated with the individual and with lack, and proceeded to rethink the concept of desire. These divergences are obviously directly linked to questions of sexuality but they also speak more broadly to some central differences between Deleuze's and Foucault's work when it comes to questions of power. In Deleuze's view, and as he argues in *Foucault*, Foucault's focus on power relations in his first sexuality book creates an impasse that incapacitates the possibility of resistance, whereas for Foucault, this focus is exactly what enables him, especially in the second and third books on the history of sexuality, to develop a relevant theory of biopower.[75]

The two friends were never to see each other again. Both of them later came to express regret about this. One of Foucault's final wishes from the hospital bed before he died in June 1984 was to see Deleuze again.[76] Though this did not happen, Deleuze was invited by Foucault's partner Daniel Defert to speak at Foucault's funeral.[77] Soon after, Deleuze began a well-attended lecture series on Foucault's work at the University of Paris VIII that lasted from 1985 to 1986 as well as the writing of *Foucault* (published in 1986). This work, Deleuze has said, came from an inner need of his own, a sense of being moved by the unfinished work of his dead friend.[78] While the peak of their disagreements have often been described as a rupture, neither Deleuze nor Foucault ultimately saw this as the end of their philosophical friendship. Since they continued to exchange letters after these events and never stopped expressing admiration for each other's work, it may be better to talk about this, as Stivale does, as a distancing rather than a rupture. Deleuze himself confirms that a distancing took hold but says that it did so because other circumstances, not the disagreement itself, made them stop seeing each other, and that this physical distance created a sense of incomprehension or estrangement.[79] Deleuze uses Foucault's own definition of passion to describe his relationship to him – with strong and weak phases, incandescent, unstable, wavering – but also confirms that they were 'on the same side', having the same conception of philosophy.[80] Ultimately, he also seemed to find in Foucault that friction and inspiration so essential to friendship as he understood it. It was irrelevant how he saw him, Deleuze argues,

> as long as I have not been able really to encounter this set of sounds hammered out, of decisive gestures, of ideas all made of tinder and fire, of deep attention and sudden closure, of laughter and smiles which one feels to be 'dangerous' at the very moment when one feels tenderness – this set as a unique combination whose proper name would be Foucault.[81]

In this work on Foucault after Foucault, Deleuze also identified and developed some fruitful conceptual connections between them. We noted earlier how Deleuze picked up the notion of the fold from the Baroque and Leibniz, but it is Foucault who helped him develop a politically enabling understanding of the concept. In his book on Foucault, Deleuze discusses the way Foucault's understanding of the fold developed after the first volume of the *History of Sexuality* and took shape with the subsequent two volumes. Recognizing how, after his first book, Foucault found himself at an impasse regarding how to find a relation to oneself in relation to power and knowledge, Deleuze sees how Foucault began to move beyond this impasse in subsequent books. In the second volume he begins to develop not a theory of the subject, but a theory of the fold as a force of subjectification, as a force bending in on itself, creating points of resistance.[82] This folding enables resistance, as it produces 'a specific or collective individuation relating to an event'.[83] In the light of their joint activities – such as their 1968 political activism and their attempts to resituate the intellectual in relation to the specific struggle rather than the universal – we may see the folds of Deleuze and Foucault's friendship also as an event giving birth to new, politicized subjectivities in response to 1968, even as their surrounding society failed to do so. In a short piece published in

Les Nouvelles littéraires in 1984, Deleuze and Guattari argue that while historians are keen to restore causality to events after the fact, there is always a part of a historical event that precisely splits or breaks with such causality – a reintroduction of the possible. 'May '68', they argue, was 'more of the order of a pure event, free of all normal, or normative causality.' It opened up the possible and the production of a new subjectivity. When such events occur, society must step up and form 'collective agencies of enunciation that match the new subjectivity' – it needs to mobilize creativity and initiative to respond to the possible that the event has opened. France, Deleuze and Guattari argue, failed to do this: it 'never came up with anything for the people'. Therefore, they argue in their essay title, 'May '68 Did Not Take Place'.[84]

Unlike the failure that Deleuze and Guattari identify after the events of '68, and redeploying their formulation, we may suggest that the friendship of Deleuze and Foucault did take place in this politicized sense. Foucault is often seen as a highly political thinker while Deleuze has often been accused of not being so. Because he tended not to engage with normative political theory, tended not to directly address topics such as democracy and justice, and only later in his oeuvre began to express explicitly political concerns, Deleuze does not correspond, as Paul Patton notes, to any standard idea of a political philosopher.[85] His conception of politics is not easily identifiable as such; it is not what he himself would describe as 'majoritarian', that is, it is not primarily concerned with existing identities, parties or ideologies. Rather, his conception of politics relies exactly on the importance of dismantling such formations. But he was certainly politically engaged. Deleuze was involved not only in GIP with Foucault, in protesting against the extradition of Croissant and in signing petitions and writing interventionist articles supporting the Palestinian struggle, but in protesting against the bombing of Vietnam, the academic hostility towards and firing of homosexuals in France, the violations of human rights in Iran, the imprisonment of the Italian philosopher and activist Antonio Negri, and the First Gulf War. His interest in political change is often ascribed to his meeting with Guattari, a narrative that, Ian Buchanan and Nicholas Thoburn show, is incorrect.[86] And as we will see in the Conclusion, while both Deleuze and Guattari made sure that their political philosophy could not be 'reconfigured as a political programme',[87] Deleuze's work has been increasingly claimed by projects of political activism. Perhaps, if he had indeed written and finished his book on Marx – it was to be called *Grandeur de Marx* (*The Grandeur of Marx*) – which he flagged in an interview with Negri shortly before his death, the perception of him as a less political philosopher would have been different. Many rumours circulate regarding this supposed work in progress. Whereas some have understood Deleuze's statement as an expression of a wish one day to write such a book, some suggest that there may be a missing manuscript out there somewhere. Indeed, Gregg Lambert notes, this statement has approached the status of a 'missing gospel'.[88] And no doubt, the text would most likely generate a revisiting of Deleuze's work in the light of this more articulated political-theoretical focus.

To return to the politics of friendship, if Guattari came to bring out the more explicitly political in his joint writing with Deleuze, the friendship between Deleuze and Foucault highlights the political dimensions of Deleuze's work even where they are not immediately apparent. In his preface to Deleuze and Guattari's *Anti-Oedipus*, Foucault writes that

> the book often leads one to believe it is all fun and games, when something essential is taking place, something of extreme seriousness: the tracking down of all varieties of fascism, from the enormous ones that surround and crush us to the petty ones that constitute the tyrannical bitterness of our everyday lives.[89]

But looking also at the way Foucault makes concepts such as the fold into political tools for imagining resistance, we can see how their joint thinking was an act of politicization. Reading Deleuze with Foucault helps bring out political dimensions of the former's work. The thinking that the friction between Deleuze and Foucault engendered in the folds of their friendship unfolds and refolds in their lives and works.

Claire Parnet also came to play an important role in the Deleuzian folds of friendship and writing. A former student of Deleuze's from Vincennes, Parnet was to collaborate with him on two projects: *Dialogues*, published in 1977 (*Dialogues*, 1987), and the televised conversations of *L'Abécédaire* (1988–9). Parnet was Deleuze's personal friend and, as Stivale notes, their collaborations evince a clear sympathy. In them, we can also see something of Deleuze's joy and commitment to students – his wish to serve as a mediator, not instructing so much as facilitating the linking of concepts that he sees as the essential role of philosophy.[90] Deleuze's generosity towards students and younger scholars has often been underlined. Schrift recalls, for example, meeting Sarah Kofman, whose work Deleuze supervised at one point, shortly before she died in 1994. Among other mementos on her desk, Kofman showed him a postcard from Deleuze that she had received in 1972 and on which he told her how much he had enjoyed reading her book *Nietzsche et la métaphore*.[91] Deleuze and Parnet's joint work was more sustained, and both their collaborative works are characterized by their attempt to write beyond the idea of a writer's identity. Their work in *Dialogues* intersects with and contributes to Deleuze and Guattari's furthering of their non-hierarchal, non-identitarian collaboration as it came to take shape in *A Thousand Plateaus*.[92] It is, perhaps, also in Deleuze and Parnet's work that this project, in its fundamental reliance on the relation between friendship and thinking, comes across most clearly. *Dialogues*, Stivale suggests, constitutes 'a constant and deliberate attempt to displace the writers' identities, as a result of which certain glimmers of an in-between of thought come to the fore through the folds of friendship, that is, through the resonances, differences, and repetitions available only within the intimacy of mediation.'[93]

Where Deleuze and Parnet's collaborations demonstrate how the directly dialogic becomes a writing in between, the relation between Deleuze and Derrida falls rather into a category of contemporary French philosophers who often, as Stivale notes, seized upon more or less distant relationships to establish a 'community of friends of thought'.[94] The connections that Kaufman outlines among thinkers such as Bataille, Maurice Blanchot, Deleuze, Foucault and Klossowski are not just a 'delirium of praise' but a serious effort to think together, 'an ecstatic breakdown of identity that occurs when it is no longer discernable what thought belongs to whom.'[95] And indeed, the gestures that recur in Deleuze's descriptions of his closer friendships with Guattari and Foucault recur, also, in Derrida's eulogy of Deleuze, published in the Parisian newspaper *Libération* after Deleuze's death in 1995. It is quite telling, maybe of Derrida's more arche-textually inclined work more generally, but also of the nature of his friendship with Deleuze, that whereas Deleuze conjures up the gesture as that which blends the physical, the intellectual and the emotional folds of his friendships with Guattari and Foucault, the gesture Derrida evokes is more directly textual. The gesture serves to try to capture the similarities in his and Deleuze's manners of writing and reading: 'a nearly total affinity' that happens 'across very obvious distances'.[96] The distances Derrida refers to pertain mainly to their philosophical approaches, which, although they had common interests, differed widely in their application.

There was also at least partly a physical distance at play in Deleuze and Derrida's friendship. Although they met repeatedly, at academic events and also slightly more private ones – Derrida recalls, for example, them driving back to Paris together after a doctoral defence, and he also remembers more physical elements of his friend: his laughter, his whispers, his raspy voice – they never worked together in the way Deleuze and Guattari or Deleuze and Foucault or Deleuze and Parnet did. That Derrida expresses, in the famous phrase from his eulogy, loneliness after Deleuze's death at the same time as he acknowledges that the conversation never quite took place – 'I will have to wander all alone in this long conversation we should have had together' – points to the sense of a fleeting, unfulfilled potential. They belonged to the same generation and yet, and especially with hindsight, we can see how not only their philosophical approaches but their ways of working differed widely. Unlike Deleuze, who rarely travelled, Derrida travelled and taught extensively abroad. Derrida was also more deeply involved in institutional politics, notably by being co-founder of the Collège international de philosophie in Paris in 1983. Still, Derrida was clearly well acquainted with Deleuze's work and he has also suggested that Deleuze was one of those in their generation to whom he felt closest.[97] The folds of friendship between Deleuze and Derrida, it has been noted, were characterized by a perception of charm, a sense of opening something in each other, of learning from each other in a deeper philosophical sense.[98] As Derrida puts it, Deleuze gave him and many of their generation 'the chance to think, thanks to him, by thinking about him'.[99]

So it seems, then, that when we talk or think about Deleuze, even in relation to the works he wrote 'on his own', we must always imagine a multitude. This is important not because we need or should try to ascertain exactly which thought comes from whom, but because we will understand both Deleuze's life and his work better if we see how it is populated by encounters. Deleuze evoked a solitude in working, but one that is 'extremely populous':

> You encounter people (and sometimes without knowing them or ever having seen them) but also movements, ideas, events,

entities. All these things have proper names, but the proper name does not designate a person or a subject. It designates an effect, a zigzag, something which passes or happens between two.[100]

Many things happened between the many twos that we have outlined here, and even if we had access to all these points of interconnection it would be impossible within the scope of this book to account for all of them. It is also quite impossible to free up the space to thoroughly explain all the fruitful concepts that arise from these encounters.

One concept that deserves special attention, however, not only because it is arguably one of the most well known and used of Deleuze and Guattari's concepts but because it helps elucidate the sense of connectivity that underlies the creative and productive potentials of friendship for Deleuze, is the concept of desire. As part of their schizoanalytical project, Deleuze and Guattari rethink the notion of desire as it has been defined by psychoanalysis. Whereas the latter sees desire as fundamentally related to lack, Deleuze and Guattari understand desire as a force of positivity – an enhancement of life as desires connect with other desires. The experimentation with psychoanalysis that they develop in their two *Capitalism and Schizophrenia* books draws not only on Freud and Lacan but on Marx and Nietzsche. It is also inspired by the work already done by contemporaries such as Klossowski. Deleuze, as he expresses in a letter to Klossowski dated 1971, finds of immense importance the way the latter introduces desire within the infrastructure, or conversely, that he introduces the category of production into desire. This provides a way, Deleuze thinks, of getting out of the sterile parallelism between Marx and Freud, money and excrement, 'all this stupidity'.[101] Coupling Freud's libido with Marx's theories of labour power, and claiming Lacan as the first schizoanalyst – Lacan 'was the first to schizophrenize the analytic field'[102] – Deleuze and Guattari's schizoanalytic project is essentially about theorizing desire beyond Oedipus and the familial, and politicizing it as something that informs the entire social and historical field of production. Importantly, this conception of desire is not so much defined in a negation of Freud and Lacan as it is a bold and creative engagement, primarily with the latter. Indeed, while there are disagreements as to whether Deleuze and Guattari's engagement with Lacan is a positive one or not, and while their work has been misread as an outright rejection of psychoanalysis, it has also been argued that Deleuze may be 'one of Lacan's most profound, but also most independent, disciples'.[103] And indeed, while Deleuze worries that Lacan would take the critique in *Anti-Oedipus* badly, Lacan ultimately seemed to have appreciated the irreverent reading of his own work: 'What I need', he said to Deleuze in one of their few encounters, 'is someone like you.'[104]

In the spirit of connectivity, Deleuze was inspired not only by contemporary thinkers such as Klossowski and Bataille but drew from a whole series of earlier philosophers to develop this notion of desire with Guattari. He picked up elements from Kant, Spinoza, Nietzsche and Marx to construct a conception of desire that produces reality, does so without recourse to a transcendent law, and frees it from its locus in the individual.[105] The rethinking of desire from a force located in an individual who in psychoanalysis is lacking something, to a force that exists everywhere and that underlies and produces that which we then come to perceive as the individual, entails a radical reconceptualization not just of desire itself but of what the individual is. The individual is not the source of desire but its temporary effect. Deleuze and Guattari use the notion of the machinic to account for what we may perceive as individual subjects but what is really only a set of components put to work in more or less stable assemblages that run on desire – desiring-machines.

The friendships outlined here, then, are desiring-machines. The joint thinking that I have tried to describe emerged from a process of connectivity that brought together entities that were really already 'quite a crowd' and put them to work. Such assemblages not only work in the production of thinking but constitute a force to wager against the power of psychoanalysis and capitalism. The production of the individual and its relation to the family that psychoanalysis encourages not only delimits the positivity and creation of desire generally, but reinforces patterns of desiring-production and subjectivity that play right into the hands of capitalism. Keeping desire locked up in the family triangle – the daddy-mummy-me – delimits desire to fixed structures and produces the lacking subjects and their individual desires on which capitalism essentially relies. But desire 'does not lack anything', Deleuze and Guattari write, 'it does not lack its object. It is, rather, the *subject* that is missing in desire, or desire that lacks a fixed subject; there is no fixed subject unless there is repression.'[106] In this light, we can see how the politics of friendship really is a politics – it is a production of desire that exceeds the structures of the subject and the family and thereby creates desiring-machines that go beyond repression. To recognize the role of friendship in Deleuze's life is thus to recognize something fundamental about his life and his work simultaneously.

4
A Practice

Philosophy is not in a state of external reflection on other domains, but in a state of active and internal alliance with them, and it is neither more abstract nor more difficult.[1]

In Chapter One, I noted briefly how one of Deleuze's early sources of inspiration was the young literature professor Pierre Halbwachs, with whom he walked on the beaches of Normandy during the war. Of course, we cannot overhear their conversation across time and space, but we can still make use of these walks to understand something of Deleuze's engagement with literature and the arts. Having learned that Deleuze's fascination with literature emerged during these walks, and recalling yet again the notions of charm and assemblage, we can position this fascination in direct relation to his philosophy as practice. Imagine, as Halbwachs recites André Gide, Charles Baudelaire and Anatole France,[2] how the sand might move and slip under their feet, the way the sea might swell and surge, and how birds might screech above. In addition, imagine the inevitable awareness of the war and the loved ones involved, along with other elements that we cannot possibly know, and this can exemplify how thinking emerges in conjunction with a number of components from a variety of fields. Literature, sand, sea, friendship, war – these are some of the grains of which Deleuze's philosophy are made. It is not abstract – it is built around elements coming together, on thinking with, through practice. Through the concept of practice,

Left to right: Deleuze, Jean-François Lyotard, Maurice de Gandillac, Pierre Klossowski, Jacques Derrida and Bernard Pautrat at the conference 'Nietzsche aujourd'hui?', held at the Centre Culturel International de Cerisy, Cerisy-la-Salle, Normandy, 1972.

we can see how the 'in between' (outlined in the previous chapter) as a crucial dimension of friendship as philosophy recurs also in Deleuze's relation to other disciplines.

I would venture to argue that we understand very little of either Deleuze's philosophy or of his life if we do not understand the role of practice in them. We have already seen it, even if we have not discussed it as such: in the intensities emerging in the experimental body of the child addressed in the first chapter, in the buggery of philosophers outlined in the second, and in the rubbing together of uneven surfaces of friendship in the third we can see that for Deleuze, neither thinking nor being can exist separately from its surroundings. And surroundings is not even the right word here, because it emphasizes exactly the separation that the notion of practice works to overcome. This is why he needs concepts such as assemblage, machine and becoming – because they refuse this separation and underline, instead, how all forms of life, whether they come in the shape of human or nonhuman bodies, artworks, literary texts, cinema or philosophy, take shape through practices. Components come together for longer or shorter periods and come to function in various constellations. Affect plays a central role here as it mobilizes relationships at instantaneous speeds and with varying constancy. Literature, sand, sea, friendship, war: these are all components of desiring-machines. We call these machines humans, or paintings, or *To the Lighthouse*; and of course, because all these constellations function differently, we need different tools to understand them. But crucially, these machines cannot be understood as entities separate from one another, and we should not delimit what they can do by making assumptions about meaning or agency but rather explore the various ways in which they can function. This is also, to return to Deleuze's caveats regarding the author-function, an attempt to make space for creativity that is not dependent on such a function. As was the case with friendship, then, it is central that philosophy can occur only in conjunction with something outside itself: 'To get out of philosophy,' Deleuze writes, 'to do never mind what so as to be able to produce it from outside. The philosophers have always been something else, they were born from something else.'[3]

So when Deleuze writes on literature, art or cinema, he does not do so simply by applying his philosophy onto these fields. Neither does he attempt to play at being a scholar in any of them in any more conventional sense of the term. Rather, and just as he thinks with Nietzsche or Spinoza and writes with Guattari or Parnet, he invents concepts in conjunction with literature, art and cinema. The practices of such in-between spaces constitute ways of getting out of habitual groves of thinking. Habit, as I discussed in Chapter Two, is a form of repetition that stabilizes forms of being and thinking. It establishes modes of being through a repeated confirmation of the same at the expense of difference. Any practice runs the risk of getting stuck in habitual repetition. This is as true of philosophy as it is of any other discipline. Indeed, the very notion of a discipline builds on the way in which the repetition of certain practices makes them recognized and established to the point where they form a delineable field. While this is certainly a practical way of organizing universities or museums, for example, it inevitably also delimits these practices along certain lines. This is why thinking requires the outside. Considering this emphasis on the importance of the outside, we might not think of Deleuze as an interdisciplinary scholar so much as one who is inherently pre-disciplinary. This is not to say that Deleuze sees the different disciplines as the same. Indeed, if this were the case they would no longer provide each other's outside. Ideas emerge in relation to specific fields and invention occurs differently between them. Deleuze vehemently resisted the idea that philosophy could exist beyond its objects and practices: 'It is a practice of concepts', he writes, 'and it must be judged in the light of the other practices with which it interferes.'[4]

Where philosophy is the creation of concepts, art creates blocs of percepts and affects. Deleuze and Guattari understand percepts and affects as pre-individual sensations. Percepts are not the same as perceptions because they are not dependent on those who perceive them, and similarly, affects are not feelings or affections tied to the individual but exceed the individual. Therefore the work of art must be seen as 'a being of sensation and nothing else: it exists in itself '.[5] Thus, for example, Deleuze writes to Klossowski admiring a film – Pierre Zucca's *Roberte* (1979), in which his friend has played a leading role – because it 'suppresses feelings' (sentiments) in order to 'unleash the power of *affects*, in their radical difference from feelings'.[6] The pre-individual, which is so central to Deleuze's philosophy, appears in a very particular way in art and cinema. Deleuze engages directly with this pre-individual plane when he writes about art as he recognizes it, not as a form of representation with meanings to be identified by a perceiving subject but as blocs of sensation that engender encounters beyond stagnant modes of being. Deleuze's philosophy thus makes for what is essentially an anti-representational aesthetics.

In his book *Francis Bacon: Logique de la sensation* (1981; *Francis Bacon: The Logic of Sensation*, 2005), Deleuze thinks with painting by exploring sensations, forces, fields, flesh, figurations, contours, colours and lines. Bacon's work helps him think how even the presence of figurative forms and narrative relations – elements Deleuze usually associates with the delimitations of representation – does not prevent the simultaneous expression of a pictorial ligature of movement. In Bacon's work, this movement reveals the body

> beneath the organism, which makes organisms and their elements crack or swell, imposes a spasm on them, and puts them into relation with forces – sometimes with an inner force that arouses them, sometimes with external forces that traverse them, sometimes with the eternal force of an unchanging time, sometimes with the variable forces of a flowing time.[7]

In Deleuze's description, we can also see how his thinking-with art is attentive to elements specific to painting – contours, colours, lines – at the same time as it connects to a more directly philosophical interest in thinking in terms of expression rather than representation. It makes sense, therefore, to question, as do Badiou and Barbara Cassin in the preface to the French edition of Deleuze's *Bacon* book, if Deleuze really writes a book 'on' Bacon in the way one might expect from what seems to be a one-artist study. 'Who', they ask, 'is the philosopher, and who is the painter?' Reflecting the direction of the book, they suggest: 'One can certainly think painting, but one can also paint thought, including the exhilarating and violent form of thought that is painting.'[8]

Although the book on Bacon, published in 1981, stands as Deleuze's most sustained study of art, his interest in art became apparent much earlier through yet another cluster of friendships and practices. While he did not practice fiction writing, painting or film-making himself (although he did, in fact, appear in small roles in a couple of films[9]), his friendships with writers, painters and film-makers entailed active involvements with their different practices. Deleuze's friendship with the painter Gérard Fromanger, for example, was a source of collaboration and inspiration for his subsequent writing on the arts. Fromanger, who became Deleuze's friend via Fanny, had a considerable influence on Deleuze's interest in painting. Deleuze was curious about how Fromanger worked and he visited his studio repeatedly to interrogate him on his practices.[10] Two dimensions central to Deleuze's understanding of the creative process of art emerged from this exchange. To begin with, we see here his understanding of painting as anti-representational. In an exhibition catalogue Deleuze wrote for Fromanger in 1973 entitled *Fromanger, le peintre et le modèle*, he suggests that 'the painter doesn't mean anything by his work.' Writing specifically about colour, he goes on to argue that colours do not mean anything:

> green is not hope; yellow is not sadness; red is not happiness or joy. Only hot or cool, hot *and* cool. Art as machinery: Fromanger paints, that is to say, he knows how to operate his paintings. The painting-machine of an artist-engineer.[11]

A second insight he picked up from his visits to Fromanger's studio was later to become crucial to how Deleuze and Guattari theorize the process of creation in relation to philosophy as a whole. In an interview with Dosse, Fromanger recalls how Deleuze asked him how he managed to paint on a blank canvas. Fromanger's response, that the canvas was not actually blank but black 'with everything every painter has painted before me', clearly excited Deleuze, who is said to have exclaimed: 'So it's not about blackening the canvas but about whitening it.'[12] This insight is echoed quite

clearly in Deleuze and Guattari's statement two decades later in
What is Philosophy?:

> The painter does not paint on an empty canvas, and neither
> does the writer write on a blank page; but the page or canvas is
> already so covered with preexisting, preestablished clichés that it
> is first necessary to erase, to clean, to flatten, even to shred, so as
> to let in a breath of air from the chaos that brings us the vision.[13]

As the reference to the writer in this quotation suggests, the idea
of having to 'whiten' the canvas from what has come before can be
applied not just to painting but to other modes of inscription as
well. Indeed, and recalling Deleuze's approach to the history of his
own field outlined in Chapter One, it applies also to philosophy.

As many who are familiar with Deleuze's work will recognize,
this reflects a Deleuzian ontology more generally. We do not
start from nothing; we start from everything. Indeed, this idea
of whitening the canvas, picked up from a painter friend in his
studio in the 1970s, can be used to illustrate Deleuze's philosophy
of immanence more generally. The dynamics between form and
the flow of difference is expressed here through art. Just as a
painter's task is to create space on a canvas black with previous
artistic formations, the philosopher's task is to create space on a
canvas crowded by pre-existing philosophical formations. And
indeed, this is what becoming is about more generally – it is not
about the introduction of anything radically new or transcendent
but rather the affirmation of the return of difference. To return once
more to the Bacon book, 'What we will call a "fact" is first of all the
fact that several forms may actually be included in one and the same
Figure, indissolubly, caught up in a kind of serpentine, like so many
necessary accidents continually mounting on top of one another.'[14]

Where Deleuze's engagement with painting constituted an
exploration of how colours, lines and contours help to push

thinking beyond representation, his two books on cinema, which directly followed the Bacon book, focus on what he sees as the two most central dimensions of cinema. Cinema too has colours and lines and contours but it introduces two additional parameters – movement and time. Deleuze sees how cinema, like art, opens a thinking of its own. This is particularly interesting also since cinema is a much more recent phenomenon than painting, literature or music. What is unique about cinema – the moving image – not only revolutionized visual culture but transformed thinking itself. Because of its relatively recent historical emergence, cinema makes apparent some things that are essentially true in Deleuze's philosophy as a whole: that we cannot define thinking as an abstract capacity, and, radically, that it cannot be defined as essentially human. As Claire Colebrook puts it:

> If we accept that the inventions and techniques of cinema allow us to think differently then we acknowledge that thought does not have its own inherent nature. Even machines, such as the technical possibilities of the camera, can transform thinking. Thinking, then, is not something that we can define once and for all; it is a power of becoming *and* its becoming can be transformed by what is not thinking's own.[15]

In the first cinema book, *Cinéma 1: L'Image-mouvement* (1983; *Cinema 1: The Movement-image*, 1986), Deleuze investigates what he calls the 'becoming narrative' of cinema. This development, he finds, occurred at the expense of other possible directions cinema could have taken.[16] What the movement-image brings to the surface is the rationalization of perception. A flux of images is conjoined methodically and in accordance with a recognizable, normative logic. This logic, which Deleuze calls the 'sensory-motor schema', underlines our reliance on conceptions of causality, consistency and truth. It is a process of regulation: a regulation of chaos by a rational linking of images. The sensory-motor schema keeps our perception of the world within predetermined routes. This sensory-motor schema is characteristic of pre-war cinema but it also continues to dominate the narrative logic of contemporary mainstream cinema. However, as Deleuze argues in his second cinema book *Cinéma II: L'Image-temps* (1985; *Cinema 2: The Time-image*, 1989), post-war cinema makes it apparent that our reliance on logic and truth took a radical blow with the Second World War. The confidence in rationality and explicability evinced in the movement-image was replaced here with 'situations which we no longer know how to react to, in spaces which we no longer know how to describe.'[17] Thus, the time-image emerges. Time is released from the logic of the sensory-motor schema and appears in and of itself. Here, Deleuze is inspired by what he identifies, in neorealist cinema such as that of Roberto Rossellini, Vittorio de Sica and Federico Fellini as well as in several other non-Italian directors, for example Orson Welles, as a break with the earlier sensory-motor logic. In the time-image, the linking of images is not necessarily subordinated to movement or action. This shift gives rise to new possibilities of thinking – something that is reflected in the large number of new concepts that emerge in this second book.

But Deleuze's interest in cinema started well before the years in which he wrote the cinema books. He was a frequent visitor to festivals and events organized by the film magazine *Cahiers du cinéma*, as Dosse notes, and he developed a productive friendship with one of its editors, Jean Narboni, who also taught at Vincennes. Deleuze also engaged in public debates about cinema from 1974 onwards. The link between cinema and philosophy, or the image and ideas, which he was to develop in considerable detail in the cinema books, was expressed as early as 1976 in an interview published in *Cahiers du cinéma*. Godard, he says, has a good saying: 'not a just image, just an image'. Philosophers, he suggests, should take after Godard and say, 'not the just ideas, just ideas'. Because, he maintains,

The mirror scene in Orson Welles's *The Lady from Shanghai* (1947).

the just ideas are always those that conform to accepted meanings or established precepts, they're always ideas that confirm something, even if it's something in the future, even if it's the future of the revolution. While 'just ideas' is a becoming-present, a stammering of ideas, and can only be expressed in the form of questions that tend to confound any answers.[18]

Various historical circumstances also enabled Deleuze to pursue his belief that cinema is important to philosophy on an institutional level. When the experimental University of Paris VIII at which he worked was relocated from Vincennes to Saint-Denis in 1980, the philosophy department and the film department ended up in close proximity, and possibilities to combine philosophy and cinema on a concrete level emerged. In 1981, Deleuze wrote to Guattari about how inspired he was by Bergson and that they needed to take part in the theorizing of cinema. What existed so far, he felt, was greatly mediocre.[19] In 1981, he also begun lecturing on cinema and his Tuesday morning film lectures were to continue until 1985. And although this never became the joint project with Guattari that he at that moment seemed to envision, and although the teaching of cinema put more pressure on his already poor health than he had estimated and also kept him from the writing that he was longing to do,[20] he did deliver this alternative theorization himself, with the publication of his first cinema book in 1983 and the second in 1985. These were clearly years of thinking through cinema for Deleuze.

Where Deleuze's work on cinema can thus be linked to a particular period in his life, his work on literature is scattered across his entire oeuvre. The studies devoted more directly to literary texts include the early essay on Sacher-Masoch published in 1961; his book on Proust, *Proust et les signes* (expanded and republished in 1970 as well as 1976 and translated as *Proust and Signs* in 1972 and *Proust and Signs: The Complete Text* in 2000); the development of his early, briefer study of Sacher-Masoch into the longer *Masochism: Coldness and Cruelty* in 1967; the book on Kafka, co-written with Guattari, from 1975; long essays on the playwrights Carmelo Bene in 1979 and Samuel Beckett in 1992; and the compilation of essays called *Critique et clinique* (*Essays Critical and Clinical*, 1997) from 1993. In addition, literature is used and referenced in various ways and sometimes to considerable extent in many of his other works, notably in *The Logic of Sense*, which gives Lewis Carroll's *Alice's Adventures in Wonderland* an important role in the philosophical theatre and which also includes readings of other writers such as Klossowski, Tournier and Antonin Artaud.[21]

Although Deleuze employs the work of these authors in many different ways, they, in each instance, relate to the question of life. Deleuze's conception of life is profoundly vitalist, which, simply put, means that for him, life is a force of difference. Life cannot be separated from transcendent principles that determine it but

The cinema in Saint-Léonard-de-Noblat.

must be seen, rather, as a continuous fluctuation of forms. Literary works express ways of living: 'Style, in a great writer', as he puts it, 'is always a style of life too, not anything at all personal, but inventing a possibility of life, a way of existing.'[22] True creation occurs at the point where we let go of the temptation to express ourselves as human subjects and to tell the stories we already know. In order to be able to be truly creative, a writer, or an artist, must give themselves up to the nonorganic dimensions of life, that is, life 'that can be found in a line that's drawn, a line of writing, a line of music'.[23] This way of approaching texts distinguishes Deleuze quite clearly from other methods of literary interpretation of his period. It is quite different, for example, from Derrida's deconstructive attention to the text and also, importantly, from psychoanalytical approaches. Although he was interested in situating texts in an extra-textual context, Deleuze was not interested in seeing the text as articulating symptoms pertaining to the writer or artist but as a symptom or set of symptoms pertaining directly to life. What forces are activated or held back for this particular form of life to express itself?

Deleuze's work on masochism deserves special attention here both because it is seminal in its field and because it constitutes the beginning of his critical and clinical project that was to colour much of his subsequent writing on literature. Written, as noted earlier, at a time when the works of Sade were picked up by many scholars, Deleuze's essay on 'coldness and cruelty' not only draws attention to the relatively neglected work of Sacher-Masoch, whose work was supposedly Sade's complementary opposite, but fundamentally questions this complementary opposition. The concept of sado-masochism, which has constituted an established theoretical term ever since Freud and which continues to be so today in many circles, relies, Deleuze argues, on a grave error. The conflation of what he sees as two radically different symptomatologies – sadism and masochism – rests on a prejudice that can be disproved if we return to the literary projects from which these terms arose. Paying sufficient attention to the works of Sacher-Masoch and Sade disrupts the dialectic on which sadomasochism relies and brings out, instead, the differential mechanisms at play. Through this strategy, he states, 'we are questioning the very concept of an entity known as sadomasochism.'[24] For those interested in the field and/or practices pertaining to them, *Masochism: Coldness and Cruelty* is an important text to discover, and it can be done so also without prior knowledge of Deleuze's philosophy, but for now, let us simply pick up the keys that this early text gives us to Deleuze's use of literature more broadly. Essentially, and as summarized by Gregg Lambert, the critical and clinical project relies on three main tenets: 1) writers are sometimes better diagnosticians of life than clinicians, 2) as a consequence of the first, certain literary works produce a 'symptomatology', that is, a set of signs indicating shifts in the arrangement of language, as well as labour and life, and 3) as a consequence of the second, certain writers can diagram potential resistance to such arrangements.[25] Reading literature according to these tenets is thus related to questions of culture, politics and, as we will return to in the next chapter, life itself.

Proust and Signs evinces another way of pursuing this project. Where the study of Sacher-Masoch brings out the distinction between the critical and the clinical more directly, since masochism has been claimed as a clinical diagnosis, Deleuze's work on Proust shows how he links word and symptom more generally. For Deleuze, divisions between signifier and signified create a mistaken separation between expression and world. This is a rather crucial element to understanding Deleuze's critique of representation. As long as we are stuck within a regime of representation whereby words simply represent things along the vectors of signifiers and signifieds, we miss the fact that words have a direct effect on these things. In fact, he suggests, signs '*do not have objects as their direct referents*' but are rather 'states of bodies (affections) and variations of power (affects)'.[26] In other words, signs emerge directly from the material: 'The biologists would be right if they knew that bodies in themselves are already a language. The linguists would be right if they knew that language is always the language of bodies. Every symptom is a word, but first of all every word is a symptom.'[27] Interpretation is not so much about learning what things mean but about seeing how they express themselves.

We have seen how the time-image in cinema can challenge the conventional modes of perception characteristic of the sensory-motor schema. For Deleuze, literature too has the ability to confirm or disrupt habitual groves of thinking. 'Writing', he and Parnet suggest, 'is very simple. Either it is a way of reterritorializing oneself, conforming to a code of dominant utterances, to a territory of established states of things: not just schools and authors, but all those who write professionally, even in a nonliterary sense', or 'it is becoming'.[28] In terms of reterritorialization, three major threats to the creative potential of literature can be identified. To begin with, and not unlike the sensory-motor schema in cinema, Deleuze sees narrative structures as potentially narrowing down expression insofar as they rely on and maintain conventional conceptions of temporality and causality. Thus, he frequently favours more experimental narratives. Second, psychoanalytic models of representation and interpretation pose dangers to literature. If one writes simply 'to recount one's memories and travels, one's loves and griefs, one's dreams and fantasies', one, in fact, commits a sin – it is 'the same thing to sin through an excess of reality as through an excess of the imagination.' This is because what happens with this kind of writing is that we remain stuck in Oedipal structures, which are then projected onto the real.[29] Literature should be evaluated in accordance with the extent to which it blocks or affirms life. Literary works that keep life caught in established modes of organization fail to perform literature's task: to open life to the impersonal. A third threat to the creative potential of literature is that it perpetually runs the risk of imitation and commercialization. In a conversation with Antoine Dulaure and Parnet published in 1985, Deleuze identifies a crisis in literature whereby it is becoming an exercise in unproductive imitation designed to please the market. Instead of productive contradictions, literature involves 'selling people what they expect: even what's "daring", "scandalous", "strange", and so on falls into the market's predictable forms.'[30]

If, on the other hand, literature produces a becoming, it means 'becoming something other than a writer, since what one is becoming at the same time becomes something other than writing'.[31] This is literature as 'the possibility of life',[32] literature as an invention of 'a people who are missing', literature as health.[33] For Deleuze, the possibility of life emerges as literature opens up ways of existing beyond territorialized structures – the people who are missing are such because they cannot be recognized by territorialized structures. 'Health' emerges here because while territorializing structures suffocate life, the breaking with them reintroduces breathing. A literature that manages to do this is a minor literature. Minor literature, which has an implicit function throughout Deleuze's writing on literature, is developed as a concept more systematically with Guattari in their *Kafka: Toward a Minor Literature*. Here, they outline three main characteristics of a minor literature: 1) its language is deterritorialized, that is, freed up from conventions regarding its meanings and representations, 2) everything about it is political; unlike a major literature, which focuses on the individual and lets the social serve as mere background, a minor literature connects the individual directly to the political, 3) everything has collective value; this is also related to the political, as individuated statements are downplayed in favour of the forging of a collective consciousness and sensibility.[34] Importantly, a minor literature is not necessarily one found in a minor language or a smaller country – indeed, one of Deleuze and Guattari's main examples, apart from Kafka, is the American canonical author Herman Melville. Rather, a minor literature is one that picks up and follows lines of deterritorialization that exist but that are oppressed in major formations of language and literature; 'To be a sort of stranger *within* [one's] own language.'[35]

While Deleuze thus engaged with art, cinema and literature in longer pieces of writing, he never wrote about music in the same sustained fashion. This does not, however, mean that music is not important to his work. One central way in which it is important is in holding a key place in understanding the relation between art and the natural world.[36] The concept of the refrain brings the two together. When Deleuze discusses music, centrally with Guattari in *A Thousand Plateaus*, he sees how music, while relying on the refrain, is also, as a creative practice, the deterritorialization of the refrain. Here Deleuze and Guattari are greatly inspired by the contemporary French composer and ornithologist Olivier Messiaen, whose interest in composition and birdsong generated compositional practices experimenting with rhythm and refrains. We can also see these ideas under further development in a letter sent by Deleuze to Clément Rosset in 1983. Deleuze writes that he is inspired by Rosset's thoughts on the relation between music, birdsong and the galloping of horses, and also that he is eager to follow it up: 'If we can make the gallop and the refrain work together,' he writes, 'this would suit me very well. It would give me all I need.'[37]

Within any given milieu, Deleuze and Guattari note, relations between organisms are established via rhythmic patterns. Indeed, in a sense, the refrain is the beginning of everything – starting from chaos, the refrain creates more or less subsistent milieus and formations. Organisms are themselves to some extent shaped by these patterns. Organisms and species have different degrees of autonomy and therefore rely on the refrain in different ways and to varying extents. The refrain establishes territories; melodies, such as for example birdsong, mark a milieu by means of the repetition of a refrain. Certain species rely for their very existence on the maintenance of a certain environment, and for them the refrain functions to secure a spatial territory. Other species – like the human – may not require a specific spatial territory in the same way, but they too rely on the refrain to ward off the chaos of the world. Thus, for example, a child alone and afraid in the dark comforts itself by humming and thereby creates a sense of stability in the midst of a sense of chaos.[38] In other words, we create security by means of such refrains. We ward off difference. The refrain, as Buchanan puts it, 'is our means of erecting, hastily if needs be, a portable territory that can secure us in troubled situations'.[39] For Deleuze, the refrain helps elucidate how different formations of life are established and how some are more consistent than others.

It shows us how formations depend on territorialization through repetition, and that they therefore also always contain the potential of becoming-other through deterritorialization.

Apart from employing it to think of the composition of the natural world, Deleuze and Guattari also discuss the refrain in relation to music understood in its more conventional forms. As described above, music, while relying on the refrain as a component, is also potentially a deterritorialization of the refrain. Unlike birdsong, music no longer relies on a specific geographical territory but creates a 'plane of composition' all of its own. In music, the hums and vibrations of sound are freed from a specific territory and thereby become a mobile territory of sorts. Different musical styles and periods, such as classicism, Romanticism and modernism, express the world differently by their differential compositions of the relations between chaos, milieu and territory. Through music, the personal and the nonpersonal are intermingled and create planes of composition that are expressive rather than representational, singular rather than subjective.[40] In *Pourparlers* (1990; *Negotiations*, 1995), Deleuze describes how he and Guattari tried to make the refrain, or the ritornello, into one of their key concepts, 'relating it to territory and Earth, the little and the great ritornello'.[41] Music is also evoked when envisioning the composition of his philosophy-as-practice as a whole: 'we really have to see philosophy, art, and science as sorts of separate melodic lines in constant interplay with one another.'[42] Deleuze also experimented with this interplay in a concrete fashion, following his former student and good friend Richard Pinhas to his studio once in 1972 to read Nietzsche to Pinhas's musical composition.[43]

As we can see, then, Deleuze's encounters with art, cinema, literature and music constituted different ways of pursuing philosophy as practice. Different modes of expression enable different modes of becoming and deserve attention for the differential ways in which they harbour the capacity to delimit as well as liberate life. While many of Deleuze's contemporary philosophers were also interested in the arts, his approach has little in common with many other philosophical preoccupations of the time. There are many reasons for this and they can be found both in his personal and his philosophical and professional inclinations. A first one is his interest in philosophers that, as I noted in Chapter Two, were not particularly in vogue at the time; this also positions Deleuze at odds with many contemporary preoccupations. From the 1960s onwards, many of his French and European colleagues were much invested in Marxist theory, psychoanalysis, phenomenology, linguistics and deconstruction, and although he was to offer his own take on these fields, his work did not sit well with any of them. Indeed, it has been suggested that Deleuze's insistent focus on metaphysics may even shock those who associate contemporary French and continental philosophy with an 'overcoming' of metaphysics.[44]

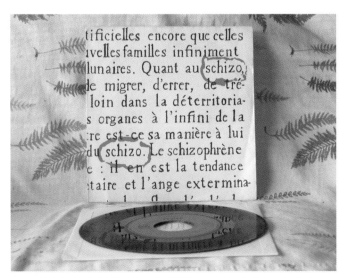

Music and deterritorialization; 'Le Voyageur/Torcol', a single released by the band Schizo, formed by Richard Pinhas in 1972.

If Deleuze was a little at odds with contemporary French and European preoccupations of the time, he also did not fit very well into the idea of and growing interest in Continental philosophy in a North American context. To begin with, there was no market in America for European works on the history of philosophy, much of which still remains untranslated, and Deleuze's early writing on thinkers such as Kant, Spinoza and Nietzsche did not become of interest until much later, after Deleuze had become popular. Second, and more centrally, Deleuze's distance from Heidegger and from the phenomenological tradition more generally constituted, as Schrift points out, a major reason why his work was not 'discovered' alongside other European colleagues in North America, despite the increasing attention it paid to Continental philosophy in a post-1960s setting. The North American interest in Continental philosophy was heavily shaped by Heidegger's work and it therefore largely remained blind to versions of European philosophy that did not invest in this tradition. In fact, the influence of Heidegger was rather limited in France at this point, but the great attention given to his work and to phenomenology in North America at the time resulted in something of an equation, in North America, between French philosophy and Sartre and Derrida. Thus, while it generally took five to ten years before Derrida's early work was translated into English (while his later work was often translated immediately after or even before its publication in French), Schrift notes, it took three or four times as long for Deleuze's work to be translated. This lopsided attention to 'French philosophy' excluded not only Deleuze (and disregarded his important role in this philosophy in France) but many other philosophers in this tradition. For example, the difficulties in assimilating his work into the phenomenological tradition also entailed a delay in American academics coming to recognize Foucault as part of the Continental philosophical tradition, despite his influential position in philosophy in France during this period.[45]

Another reason for the lack of recognition of Deleuze's work during this period may have been his lack of interest in travelling to and working in the U.S. In preferring to stay put, he stood out among French contemporaries who were increasingly travelling and partaking in a North American context. Lyotard, Serres, Bruno Latour and Michel de Certeau all spent time teaching at the University of California, San Diego, in the 1970s; Foucault taught at the University of California, Berkeley, in the early 1980s; and Derrida at the University of California, Irvine, from the mid-1980s onwards. Deleuze was not very interested in travelling or in being a public intellectual. He did not travel much and did not attend many academic conferences. This can be explained in part by his health problems – he had lung problems throughout most of his life – which prevented travel or made it very difficult for him to find the energy. But he has also admitted that being in a position to decline travel because of health reasons was one of the perks of being ill.[46] He did not like travelling and found the idea of it a false start, at least as a mode of enhancing your thinking: 'Travelling is going somewhere else to say something and coming back to say something here.' And in terms of being a public intellectual, he claimed he was not one because he did not have a ready-made stock of thoughts and views at ready supply. All he felt he could talk about was what he was writing about, when he was writing about it – a few years later even this was gone, or at least he would have to learn it again from the beginning.[47] This may seem contradictory – on the one hand believing that thought occurs 'in between', as has already been stressed repeatedly, and on the other hand resisting the idea of travel and intellectual exchange. But Deleuze's idea of communication and travel builds on the idea of making space for them, not by going through the motions but, quite the contrary, by emptying ourselves of such purposeful movement. He says in an interview with Parnet that what we suffer from is not 'any lack of communication, but rather from all the forces making us say things when we've nothing much to say'.[48]

Deleuze's first and only visit to North America was effectuated by Sylvère Lotringer, a French academic activist and founding editor of the journal and editing venture Semiotext(e) in the U.S. Joining the faculty at Columbia University in the early 1970s, Lotringer and Semiotext(e), which actively brought French theory, activism and the American avant-garde together, came to play an important role in the integration of French theory into North America. A great appreciator of Deleuze and Guattari's *Anti-Oedipus* and also a sometime collaborator of Guattari, Lotringer managed to lure the rather reluctant Deleuze to participate in what ended up being a legendary 'Schizo Culture' conference, which Lotringer organized at Columbia in 1975. The conference brought together French theorists such as Deleuze and Guattari, Foucault and Lyotard with American writers and musicians such as William Burroughs and John Cage. Although the symposium came to play an important role in the introduction of Deleuze's work to a North American audience, the event itself, François Cusset notes, was not exactly successful. Deleuze, as well as Guattari and Foucault, was met with hostility from members of the audience. Foucault was accused by a member of the audience of being paid by the CIA and Ti-Grace Atkinson, a writer, philosopher and radical feminist, accused them all of being 'phallocrats'.

Refusing to take further part in the event – the 'last counter-cultural event of the 60s', Foucault is supposed to have called it – the Frenchmen found a guide in the artist and activist Jean-Jacques Lebel, who introduced them to counter-culture poets, singers and editors such as Allen Ginsberg, Bob Dylan, Joan Baez and Lawrence Ferlinghetti. Lebel also took them to a Patti Smith concert and to meet with members of the Black Panthers.[49] But Deleuze's interest in American counter-culture existed before this brief visit to the West. Although he was not physically working with the other French theorists in California, where, as Cusset describes it, the borders between the counter-culture and the university were blurred for a while in 'a zone in which artistic experimentation and innovative courses on theory began to resonate with one another',[50] Deleuze frequently references figures like Ginsberg, Cage and Burroughs. His work, especially that with Guattari, was, as Dosse notes, in turn picked up by counter-cultural artists.[51] He also thought highly of American literature more generally. One of the seemingly contradictory aspects of his life and work is that while he, as we have just seen, thought so little of travelling himself and so rarely subjected himself to it, he appreciated American literature precisely for its geographical negotiations: 'the flight towards the West, the discovery that the true East is in the West, the sense of the frontiers as something to cross, to push back, to go beyond. The becoming is geographical.' For this, he argues, France has no equivalent. Compared with the movement and deterritorialization and leaps of Anglo-American literature, the French, he insists, 'are too human, too historical, too concerned with the future and the past'.[52]

Yet another related reason for the delay in the North American reception of Deleuze as compared to his contemporary French colleagues is, Cusset maintains, that this reception was shaped by 'two decades of misunderstandings'. The early translations of Deleuze's books on Proust and Sacher-Masoch created an impression of him as a cross between an unconventional literary critic and an alternative sexologist; early and rather fleeting uses of his work, such as that by Fredric Jameson, made him come across as a postmodern aesthete; leftist periodicals celebrated his work as being in the spirit of Wilhelm Reich and Herbert Marcuse; and *Anti-Oedipus* was cited within a critique of the colonial and heterosexual subject.[53] Still, and what also needs mentioning here, is the rather sceptical reception Deleuze's work was given by the second-wave feminists active during this period. We have already seen how Deleuze and Guattari's appearance at the schizoanalysis conference in 1975 was interrupted by hostility on behalf of feminists in the audience. Alice Jardine's 'Woman in Limbo: Deleuze and His Br(others)', published in

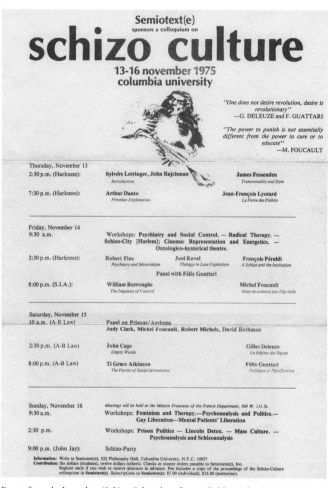

Poster from the legendary 'Schizo Culture' conference held at Columbia University in 1975.

SubStance in 1984, constitutes a good example of the reluctance and even hostility of academic feminists during this period, warning, as it does, feminists from engaging with these thinkers' work. A more general feminist scepticism concerning the devaluation of the

Deleuze on the beach in Big Sur, California, in 1975.

concept of the subject was taking place in theory during this period
– just at a time, it was argued, when women were finally getting close
to acquiring a subject position to begin with. It was hard for feminists
working towards autonomy and self-determination to see how a
Deleuzian micropolitics would be helpful. As Jardine's article shows,
the concept of becoming-woman, originally one of Guattari's concepts
but one that he and Deleuze continued to develop together, came
across as particularly provoking.

Centrally, becoming-woman is a concept that Deleuze and
Guattari position as the very beginning of the process of becoming.
Because man has always been positioned as the starting point and as
the subject position from which all else is measured, all becomings
must first pass through a becoming-woman. This is the first step
towards escaping the logic of subjectivism. As we will see in the
concluding chapter, this concept, as well as the productive potential
of Deleuze's philosophy for a feminist project more generally, came
to be appreciated to an increasingly large extent later on, but when
it first hit the North American context, it was perceived as highly

disturbing. Becoming-woman, Jardine maintained, constitutes but yet another attempt to make women into an abstraction and to capture woman 'in a whirling sea of male configurations'.[54] Judith Butler was also decidedly sceptical, taking issue with another central Deleuzian concept, that of desire. As we will see, it took until the early 1990s before feminist thinkers, including notably Rosi Braidotti and Elizabeth Grosz, really began to see the point of Deleuze's philosophy. This is largely also when his work came to be appreciated and employed as a form of practice – in active conjunction with, rather than for, against or after, Deleuze.

Not only do we need to recognize the centrality of practice to Deleuze's philosophy to understand it, as I hope to have shown in this chapter, we also need to remember this centrality in any subsequent engagement we may want to have with his work. The many concepts that pour generously from his writing seem to lend themselves so easily to application. The cinema books, with their taxonomical ambition, are particularly susceptible here for what could easily become a rather inactive and nonthinking method of application. Therefore, we need to recall that a practice is a living activity, one that does not copy but that creates. A Deleuzian practice must be based on an adequately irreverent stealing, a stealing that 'is the opposite of plagiarizing, copying, imitating, or doing like. Capture is always a double-capture, theft a double-theft, and it is that which creates not something mutual, but an asymmetrical block, an a-parallel evolution.'[55] We can never steal Deleuze the way he stole Guattari, but we can, perhaps, invent our own ways of stealing.

5
A Life

It's organisms that die, not life. Any work of art points a way through for life, finds a way through the cracks.[1]

'It is hard', as Laura Cull puts it, to 'imagine that Deleuze was ever able to forget his body.'[2] In his mid-twenties, he was already suffering from respiratory problems. At the end of the 1960s, a hard-beaten tuberculosis returned and destroyed one of his lungs. Hospitalized just before his doctoral defence in the late 1960s, he nonetheless managed to go through with this academic trial, albeit in an abridged form. Afterwards, he had to undergo an operation that left him with only one lung and respiratory problems for the remainder of his life.[3] When he describes this major surgery in a letter to Klossowski, Deleuze calls it 'a cowardly organic aggression'.[4] As we will see in this chapter, and as Deleuze's condition deteriorated through the years, he came to develop rich conceptions of health, fragility, illness and exhaustion. He also, with Guattari, developed a complex conception of the body. But while Deleuze as a painfully embodied philosopher reminds us of the persistence of embodied thought in his philosophy, we must also note that he was never very interested in the personal body as such. For him, the organism has certain forms and functions and depends upon certain habits and social identities. It is determined not only by biological functions, but by cultural, historical and political values, a central one of which is the Oedipal relations to which it is ascribed. This body in the most conventional sense of the term effects an overcoding of what is really an intensive desiring-production that connects beyond social or habitual determinations. This intensive connectivity is a movement on the 'body-without-organs', the rising and falling of intensities; it is life itself that is not delimited by preset forms, be they philosophical, psychoanalytical, social or political. It is immanence, a life.[5]

'A life' is a concept that brings together all the most central tenets of Deleuze's philosophy. It is a concept with its own texture, a texture that in turn underlies all his other concepts. 'Life is not your history,' write Deleuze and Claire Parnet; life is charm. This charm emerges in unique and momentary combinations. And as we have seen, Deleuze's life gives witness to these combinations and their various components: individuations, friendships, literature, art: 'through each fragile combination a power of life is affirmed.'[6] This is why philosophy had to be a practice for Deleuze and Guattari and why it had to centre around the creation of concepts. As difference slows down to the point where it approximates identity, a distinction is created between inside and outside; but if we accept these formations as closed, that is, accept that identity is really possible, we prevent ourselves from seeing the differential dynamics of life. A concept captures and helps analyse a certain formation of life at a certain point, but if we persist in clinging to the same concepts, we presume that formations remain the same. We deny life its expressive nature. This sheds further light on Deleuze's apprenticeship to philosophy, as discussed in Chapter Two. Even if earlier philosophers may have been 'right' in various ways, their work needs to be brought back to life by becoming active. It also sheds more light on Deleuze's philosophy of friendship and of practice, as we can see how he was working to shake any ground that may have settled under his own or others' feet by opening life up again to difference.

To be creative, life needs to be active, that is, it needs to free itself not only from molar constructions such as the concept of the subject or the author but from all reactive forces that bind it in present structures. Here, Deleuze builds on Nietzsche's distinction between active and reactive forces and sees how life forms emerge in constant negotiation between them. Active forces are the dominant ones, to which reactive ones are bound to respond. This means that while the former have the power to create new connections, the latter only have power to respond to – to negate or confirm or modulate – connections already staked out. While an active force is an affirmation of difference, a reactive force confirms or negates only what it recognizes, and as such it imposes limits and restrictions on the active – on life.[7] The problem is, he suggests, that we 'always think we have done enough when we understand an organism in terms of reactive forces'.[8] Deleuze's interest in philosophy as well as in literature, art and cinema is based on the extent to which they do more than simply represent life; that is, the extent to which they express an active force that does more than just confirm or negate the same. This strategy of affirmation and difference applies to all levels of life for Deleuze, including his own philosophical practice. We are strong, he writes to Guattari, because we build our work not on being anti, but rather on a conception of the positive.[9]

Thus, having little patience with the anti or the polemic – for they ultimately fail to create anything new – Deleuze had all the more belief in laughter and humour as great forces of life. Humour has an affirmative power in that it allows for the uncertainty of the self and of truth. 'A great author', he says in reference to Proust, 'is someone who laughs a lot.'[10] Unlike irony, which remains within the logic of the individual and identity, humour is coextensive with the nonsense that suspends signification. It opens up a space for experimentation that is not possible if we take ourselves too seriously.[11] Laughter, as a physical instantiation of humour, is important also because it provides an embodied yet impersonal expression of joy. We have already seen how laughter was repeatedly evoked in the context of Deleuze's friendship with Foucault. We have also noted how Deleuze's own laughter lingered in the memory of Derrida. And laughter is a recurring feature both as a reference in Deleuze's writing and as part of his friendships, not least as a repeated occurrence in his dialogues with Parnet.[12] Unless it is of the knowing or derisive kind, and as such initiated as a reactive response, laughter promotes an affirmative and active mode of engagement with thinking. This is not because philosophy should be taken lightly but because philosophers should take themselves lightly; they must allow for mistakes, for nonsense, for the openness of experimentation. The importance of laughter is one that Deleuze developed not only in relation to contemporaries and friends such as Foucault and Parnet but also, as Stivale notes, in relation to earlier writers and thinkers including Proust, Spinoza and, most centrally perhaps, Nietzsche. The latter emphasizes the value of laughter, warns against non-laughing men, and impels the Higher Men to '*learn* – to laugh!'[13] For Deleuze, laughing and dancing 'beyond yourself' means opening yourself up to forces of life that unsettle reactive formations. Laughter has an intimate and decidedly physical relation with such experimentation, and so have writing and art to the extent that they too evoke affective responses that go beyond what the subject recognizes on a rational level.

For Deleuze, this physical dimension of life as an active force associated with laughter is also evoked in relation to illness and health. Life is linked to what may seem like an oppositional couple but is actually a complementary one: fragile health and 'Great Health'. While often haunted by ill-health, many thinkers 'carry life to the state of absolute power'.[14] There is no room for neurosis in Great Health – 'I am', Deleuze writes in a letter to Villani, 'disgusted, theoretically and practically, by any kind of complaint regarding life, by any tragic culture.'[15] Nietzsche constitutes a key example of a thinker who was of ill-health but was also very much alive.[16] Nietzsche also conceptualized this in *The Gay Science*, where he outlines 'the *great health*', 'a new health, stronger, more seasoned, tougher, more audacious, and gayer'.[17] Another example of this combination of fragile and Great Health Deleuze found in the French chanteuse Edith Piaf, whom he greatly admired and whom he describes as singing with a productive imbalance even as she was falling apart, taking on slightly off-key notes and making them work.[18] This is style at its best for Deleuze. Creativity emerges in the cracks, but only if you let the cracks themselves speak and not your ideas about them. 'You don't write with your ego, your memory, and your illnesses,' he writes; 'In the act of writing there's an attempt to make life something more than personal, to free life from what imprisons it.'[19] And as Deleuze's philosophical works show, he did not write with his illness but with what comes across as a persistent pursuit of life and health, not on a personal level so much as on the level of thinking. For him, health is that which opens up life beyond its determinations, that which invents 'a people who are missing'.

Health in the 'dominant and substantial' sense of the individual, on the other hand, may even prevent the encounters with life that a delicate health enables.[20] It is when we are forced to question our habitual ways of being and thinking about ourselves and our bodies, for example through illness, that those habits are exposed exactly as such. Without romanticizing the idea of illness – and indeed Deleuze's long-term and increasingly severe suffering speaks directly against such an impulse – it does constitute one way of challenging relations between bodies, understood here in a wider sense of both human and nonhuman entities.[21] For Deleuze, the affirmation of the active forces that are essential to Great Health necessarily means abandoning reactive ideas about what an organism consists of. Freeing life from that which imprisons it is largely about recognizing and affirming these aspects of our 'selves', a term that now has to be bracketed because it must be remodelled in this very process. This is vitalism for Deleuze, a theme that he recognizes as perhaps the single most important one uniting his predecessors Spinoza, Nietzsche and Bergson. Vitalism is an affirmation of the active force of life as it expresses itself in ways also not always familiar to us. Identity is a dead end here:

> We have to counter people who think 'I'm this, I'm that', and who do so, moreover, in psychoanalytic terms (relating everything to their childhood or fate), by thinking in strange, fluid, unusual terms: I don't know what I am – I'd have to investigate and experiment with so many things in a non-narcissistic, non-oedipal way – no gay can ever definitively say 'I'm gay'. It's not a question of being this or that sort of human, but of becoming inhuman, of a universal animal becoming –not seeing yourself as some dumb animal, but unraveling your body's human organization, exploring this or that zone of bodily intensity, with everyone discovering their own particular zones, and the groups, populations, species that inhabit them.[22]

One way in which Deleuze works to approach life without getting caught in reactive formations is by celebrating verbs, especially in the infinitive form. Verbs brush off the personal and the stability of being by simultaneously underlining the impersonal and the becoming inherent in all things. In this form, life is expressed as movement. To laugh, to dance, to arrive – the infinitive verb points to an event without delimiting its components to a subject and his or her actions. In *The Logic of Sense* he famously outlines the importance of verbs in relation to *Alice's Adventures in Wonderland*. The proper name maintains the illusion of fixed personal identity, but Alice is 'swept away by the verbs' and enters into pure becoming. The present is eluded in favour of a process without a stable link to the past or the future – '"which way, which way?" asks Alice, sensing that it is always in both directions at the same time.'[23] This is a way for Deleuze to understand the relation between the physical and the metaphysical.[24] On the one hand, there are bodies, physical entities, 'states of affairs' – what Deleuze calls the actual – and on the other there is an incorporeal layer consisting of the impersonal effects and potentialities of these states of affairs: what he calls the virtual. These two dimensions of becoming belong to two different temporalities – Chronos, the embodied time of the present, and Aion, which just is, beyond past and future:

> If the infinitives 'to die', 'to love', 'to move', 'to smile', etc., are events, it is because there is a part of them which their accomplishment is not enough to realize, a becoming in itself which constantly both awaits us and precedes us.[25]

Verbs in their infinitive underline how we, rather than dealing with subjects and actions, deal with an interchangeability between the virtual and the actual – a folding, to return to a concept used earlier. Instead of a body that dances, a dancing body becomes dance. Through the event, it enters into a becoming, an actualization of the virtual. This is the event.

In this context, we may also want to consider the verb 'to breathe'. As Cull points out, one may see the many references to air in Deleuze's work in a different light once aware of his own very real struggle with breathing. Describing certain philosophers or events as a breath of fresh air,[26] there is a sense that the metaphor is becoming literal for Deleuze. This would also make sense in the context of Deleuze's philosophy in that the translation between figurative and literal that constitutes a metaphor does not generally sit well with him, since he, as we have seen, sees all expression as expression of life directly.[27] And although we cannot, of course, know how Deleuze perceived his own body, it seems to make sense to consider his illness in the light of his philosophy of the event and to consider the verb 'to breathe' as a very particular type of verb in its intimate relation to life and to the body. To breathe is perhaps the most intimate physical act, yet at the same time the most impersonal of all actions, the ground at once of life and *a* life. That is, 'to breathe' speaks directly to the impersonal life that, Deleuze would argue, exists as a virtual dimension of all actions, including those that may seem considerably more voluntary. Life in its pure form – 'a life' – is the affects and percepts of the virtual dimension, and an individuation is an organization of elements of this dimension in actual time.[28] Throughout his life, Deleuze had to struggle with a way of living in which this most impersonal action did not come naturally. Struggling to breathe means becoming acutely aware of breathing – it is no longer an impersonal but a highly self-conscious act. It becomes less a life that gathers its force from the virtual by being repeatedly actualized – to breathe – than one which struggles to connect to life by taking place.

On the one hand, Deleuze describes ageing and fragility as something quite useful to himself and his own projects. In the televised discussions with Parnet towards the end of the 1980s, that is, when Deleuze was in his mid-sixties, he expresses a sense of relief that comes with old age. It is a splendid age, he feels, despite the slowness that comes with it, because it releases you from the expectations, binds, plans and disappointments that characterize the younger years. They let go of you and you let go of them. You finally get the chance to just be – not be one thing or another but just to be.[29] This emphasis on being may seem contradictory in the light of his philosophy of becoming but, putting it in its context, we may see it rather as a way of expressing a mode of existence released from the more specific trajectories of those who are not yet old. On the other hand, as Deleuze got older, his illness took an increasing toll on his strength and his capacity to work: 'My health is getting worse,' he wrote in a letter to a friend in 1992, 'it is not an illness but a state which makes it constantly difficult for me to breathe: you can imagine how it changes everything, including work.'[30] Though he had been ill for several decades already, his condition was deteriorating more quickly and towards the end he was forced to spend much of his time hooked to an oxygen tank – 'like a dog'.[31]

When Guattari died in 1992, Deleuze was too ill to attend his funeral. In honour of Guattari, Dosse recounts, their joint friend, the artist Jean-Jaques Lebel (who had escorted them in the U.S.) made a sculpture out of Guattari's old car. Guattari had been a great fan of cars and Lebel made a car sculpture that included hallucinogenic mushrooms, loudspeakers projecting Guattari's voice, and a slot through which people could drop messages. He also included in the sculpture a number of oxygen tubes to represent Deleuze. Deleuze was pleased, Lebel recalls, because the artist had 'transformed' the cursed tubes.[32] In the midst of life and death, life won again, if only for a moment. But even with these cursed tubes, it gradually became harder for Deleuze to breathe and he was suffering from bad asthma attacks. Dosse's biography includes several accounts by friends recalling how horrific Deleuze's situation was. Stories of how he, in the period before his death, tried to call friends but was prevented from talking properly by his breathing problems indicate the progressive severity of the situation. Statements like 'It's hard for me to breathe' bring out the ruthlessness of his illness and possibly also a certain stoicism on his behalf. And indeed, a friend of his, Yves Mabin Chennevière, who saw him towards the end, suggests that it was due to his extraordinary courage that he bore it for as long as he did.[33]

The difficulty of working and writing was particularly hard to bear and Deleuze became increasingly frustrated and depressed. The incapacity to work, Dosse suggests, was even worse than the physical suffering.[34] That the capacity to work seems to have been almost more important to Deleuze than his health comes across also in how he discusses his former drinking habits in the interviews with Parnet. Here, he admits that he used to drink a lot – *a lot*. He says that if there is something that might justify habits that are bad for your health, such as drinking or taking drugs, it

Left to right: Hopi Lebel, Jean-Jacques Lebel, Guattari, Deleuze and Fanny, Paris, 1990.

is if they enable you to work. Conversely, he sees the real danger with such habits to be that they might prevent you from working. And although he says he had to stop drinking for health reasons, he also says that he stopped when he realized that it was actually making him lose interest in working. He thought that drinking helped him create concepts – 'it's bizarre!' – until he realized that drinking made him not want to work at all. It was at that point he realized that he needed to give it up.[35] It was also the capacity to work that he brought up with Châtelet as a reason for the latter to stay alive. Sharing the experience of severe respiratory problems with this good friend and fellow philosopher who, after a severe case of lung cancer and an ensuing tracheotomy, also had to live with the oxygen machines, Deleuze encouraged his friend to stay alive as long as he could work: 'as long as you can still hold a pen,' Châtelet's wife Noëlle recalls him saying, 'you can still live.'[36] Writing is a way of staying alive, a reason for staying alive. In this light, we can see how Deleuze's own increasing difficulties with writing must have been detrimental to his life force. And indeed, how could he aspire towards the 'Great Health' of invention and creation when his illness prevented him from writing in the first place? 'I'm working on the final version of *What is Philosophy?*', he wrote in a letter to Jean-Clet Martin in 1990, 'less like an inspired bird and more like a donkey striking itself.'[37]

In an essay on Beckett published in 1992, Deleuze discusses the difference between being tired and being exhausted as a difference between not realizing a possibility (that nonetheless remains and can be discovered after some rest) and actually having exhausted the possible: 'The tired person can no longer realize, but the exhausted person can no longer possibilize.'[38] Reading him through his own work, one can imagine that the tiredness that was a common presence in his life could for a long time be beaten back by a vitalist philosophy that both proposes and is an example of a formidable creative force and realization. Realization reappears again and again. But when no longer able to pursue this force, there is less to set against the tiredness, less to realize – and thereby also less to possibilize: 'Does he exhaust the possible because he is himself exhausted, or is he exhausted because he has exhausted the possible?'[39] Exhaustion, Deleuze writes in the same essay, is

> the most horrible position in which to await death: seated without the strength either to get up or to lie down, watching for the signal that will make us stand up one last time and then lie down forever.[40]

On 4 November 1995, Deleuze committed suicide by throwing himself out of the window of his Paris apartment. At this point, he was so ill that many have wondered how he was even able to make it to the window. The death was not completely unexpected for his close friends, who had witnessed his suffering. Not only did the difficulties of breathing and talking haunt him towards the end, but he was haunted by having witnessed the suffering and perishing of Châtelet from his lung problems. Not wanting to go through the same process as his old friend was a stated reason for his suicide.[41] Yet, many have noted that suicide seems quite irreconcilable with the philosophy of life for which Deleuze had made such a strong case. However, this act is inscribed quite explicitly within this philosophy. Addressing death and suicide directly in *Difference and Repetition*, Deleuze insists that death has two faces. There is the external and inevitable force that cancels 'large differences in extension', that is, that destroys the differences that have constructed a life in a particular organism. But there is also the internal power that 'frees the individuating elements from the form of the I or the matter of the self in which they are imprisoned.' Suicide, he argues, is an (inevitably failed) attempt to make these two faces coincide: it 'compensates for the differentiations of the I and the Self in an overall system' at the same time as it is 'a protest by the individual which has never recognised itself within the limits of the Self and the I.'[42]

What is stressed here is the crucial difference, not in kind but in form, between life as imprisoned in certain forms and life as free from such forms. The centrality of the impersonal and the singular that reappears throughout Deleuze's philosophy re-emerges here as an affirmation of the liberation from certain forms. What is stressed also are the powerful and singular forms of life generated by the temporary form of the individual. Addressing the suicide of Primo Levi, Deleuze insists that Levi 'committed suicide personally', making a distinction thereby between the life of the individual and the life forces and resistance that were liberated through his writing.[43] If we can adopt this approach in relation to Deleuze's own legacy we acknowledge his philosophy of the singular and impersonal. Perhaps he himself had exhausted the possible. The possible, in his philosophy, has a distinctly different meaning than the potential. For while the possible remains related to Chronos – to the realm of the actual – because it builds on our possibility

Deleuze ad infinitum.

to imagine a next step after the present, the potential exists in the virtual realm. Someone not exhausted can possibilize but can never potentialize. To open life towards its potential is not to imagine what may be a possible next step, but to remain open to the event – that which befalls us not from a sensible realm but from life itself. Committing suicide 'personally': this is a possible act for Deleuze the individual, within Chronos. But with his two faces of death in mind, Deleuze's death should perhaps also be seen as 'a death' – the cancellation of a specific assemblage that also opens to the potential which he was too exhausted at this point to personally imagine. Deleuze was buried in the new cemetery in his beloved Saint-Léonard-de-Noblat in Limousin on 10 November.

But before that, on 7 November – that is, only a few days after his death – the French paper *Libération* published a 'L'adieu des philosophes', a farewell to Deleuze from a number of contemporary philosophers.[44] Today we stop, writes Jean-Luc Nancy, to listen to what Deleuze called 'absolute deterritorialization'. But, recalling the central importance of production in Deleuze's work, 'tomorrow we resume the task'.[45] In a time of nihilism, writes Lyotard, Deleuze was the affirmation. 'Why do I speak of him in the past tense,' Lyotard asks himself, and imagines Deleuze's reply: 'It's your idiotic grief.'[46] Giorgio Agamben recalls a class he took with Deleuze in 1987 where he talked about self-enjoyment: 'This is not the small pleasures of being oneself' but 'a contemplation of existence that produces joy and the naive confidence that it will last and without which our hearts would stop.'[47] Of these eulogies, Derrida's is the most quoted, being also repeatedly cited in relation to theories of mourning more generally. 'So much to say', he writes, 'about the time that was allotted to me, as to so many others of my "generation," to share with Deleuze, so much to say about the chance to think, thanks to him, by thinking about him.'[48] Apart from the great respect that becomes apparent through the words of these philosophers, it is also worth noting how the two faces of death that Deleuze theorized echoes in their farewells: the combination of the personal – the very special charm that was Deleuze – with the importance of the impersonal qualities of his work, the sense of great loss that came with his death, combined with a pressing and affirmative sense of life.

It seems quite apt that Deleuze should write an essay entitled 'L'Immanence: une vie' (1995; 'Immanence: A Life', 2007) in the middle of his last and most difficult period. Published in the same year as his suicide – it was written, as John Rajchman puts it, 'in a strange interval before his own death' – this essay is sometimes seen as a testament of sorts.[49] Here, Deleuze again underlines the impersonal nature of life. '*A* life is everywhere,' he writes, 'in all the moments that a given living subject goes through and that are measured by given lived objects: an immanent life carrying with it the events or singularities that are merely actualized in subjects and objects.'[50] Looking back on the life outlined in this biography in the light of this conception of life, we could, perhaps, see the personal history of Deleuze also as a 'carrying' of events and singularities.

We can look at the 'moments' that Deleuze moved through and at the actualizations that took place throughout this journey. Perhaps we can also see the life and work as a Baroque fold, the curving and twisting of surfaces that disables identification of inside and outside. Deleuze, as many have testified and continue to testify, was an extraordinary thinker, but if there is one thing that I hope this biography has brought forth it is that his life as well as his work took place in a series of foldings and unfoldings that he would have hated to claim purely as his own, imprisoned under the auspices of a proper name.

Conclusion

> But the charm is not the person. It is what makes people be grasped as so many combinations and so many unique chances from which such a combination has been drawn.[1]

We are tempted, Nancy writes in his eulogy, in our sadness and respect, to retain Deleuze 'in a freeze frame'.[2] But this, as Nancy acknowledges, is a temptation we must resist.[3] It would not be respectful to let Deleuze's thinking stagnate, to subject it to that habitual repetition that he so persistently struggled against, to inscribe him into that history of philosophy that he worked so hard to upset. Getting to know Deleuze we might, like he once did with the representatives of the history of philosophy, begin our process of initiation by spending a lot of time painting portraits before we begin to create our own landscapes. But eventually we need to see, as did Deleuze with a little help from his friend Fromanger, that true creativity depends on the realization that the canvas is already full of layers and that our job is to work with these layers to make them express themselves differently. Deleuze as landscape. One way of navigating this landscape would be through mapping. Deleuze and Guattari were fond of maps: 'Make a map, not a tracing,' they write, and mean that unlike a tracing, which is a more passive form of reproduction, mapping involves a creative process. Whereas a tracing simply represents what seems like the stable properties of what is, a mapping is open to the many mutable and virtual dimensions that are always part of things. Making a map is an open and experimental practice that accommodates connectivity.[4] Much of Deleuze's philosophy, as we have seen, centres on such connectivity and the ways it allows for life to emerge afresh. Perpetually opening windows, he strives to make space for that breath of fresh air that can rekindle what threatens to otherwise become immobile and inactive.

Deleuze's advice to Villani, a student who wanted him to supervise his doctoral dissertation, is a case in point. While stating that he would be delighted if Villani would write on him, Deleuze also warned the student from becoming too obsessed with his work:

> I have seen many people who wanted to become the disciple of someone, and who originally were as gifted as their masters but came out sterilized from this relationship. It is terrible. Working on me has two major drawbacks: it won't help you in your academic career, which may not be essential, but is very important nonetheless, but mostly you have to write your own philosophic and poetic oeuvre, and it cannot be constrained by mine.[5]

What he is saying here, in so many words, is that there must be no Deleuzians. And indeed, 'There are no Deleuzians,' Constantin V. Boundas argues; 'there are only people using Deleuze-blocs and Deleuze diagonal lines of transformation for the sake of creating concepts in philosophy, sensations in the arts, and modes of living in ethics and politics that are not necessarily (and sometimes not at all) Deleuze's.'[6]

One may think that this would be an easy task – one easier than being a more dutiful disciple anxious to follow and affirm a master's thought – but it has proved quite a challenge to many who have come after to find a creative way of engaging with Deleuze's philosophy that is unfaithful to it in a faithful way.

As we saw in Chapter Four, during his lifetime Deleuze was not as well known outside France as many of his contemporaries, but in the new millennium his work has grown more popular than ever, especially in the English-speaking academic community. While Derrida, Foucault and Lyotard may still be more widely quoted than Deleuze, Elie During noted in the early days of the new millennium that 'Deleuze continues to gain ground in the academy as well as in larger spheres.'[7] In fact, the scholarly interest in Deleuze today is way beyond what could have been imagined in the early 1980s when Derrida, Foucault and Lyotard, as we have seen, were already being read at American universities while the translation of Deleuze's work into English had only just begun. Apart from the very early translations of *Présentation de Sacher-Masoch* into *Masochism: An Interpretation of Coldness and Cruelty* in 1971 and of *Proust and Signs* in 1972, it was only from the mid-1980s onwards that his oeuvre begins its journey in the English-speaking parts of the world. The end of the 1980s and the decade to follow saw an increase in speed in the English translation of Deleuze's work.

The last decade of the twentieth century and the first decades of the twenty-first have seen an unprecedented interest in Deleuze in an English-speaking context. The work to attain critical mass initiated at least in part by Boundas (apart from translating Deleuze's work, Boundas also organized the first international conference on Deleuze at Trent University in 1992) has virtually exploded. Quite apart from the numerous publications based on or inspired by his work, the field known as 'Deleuze studies' has grown with remarkable speed and has also become increasingly institutionalized. In 2000, Edinburgh University Press launched a book series of edited collections called *Deleuze Connections* and in 2007 it was complemented with a monograph series entitled *Plateaus: New Directions in Deleuze Studies*. That same year, the press, along with the founding editor Ian Buchanan, also launched the *Deleuze Studies* journal, which, publishing three issues per year, focuses exclusively on Deleuze's philosophy. The first International Deleuze Studies Conference took place at Cardiff University in 2008 and has since been followed by annual conferences across Europe and the United States. These conferences are typically preceded by a 'Deleuze Camp', which is a pedagogic endeavour that collects experienced and less experienced Deleuze scholars with the aim of learning more about Deleuze's thinking. Since 2013, there has also been an annual International Deleuze Studies Conference in Asia to complement the Anglo-American project.

These various initiatives have created excellent venues for the exchange, learning and dissemination of Deleuze-based scholarship. But we need also to beware of the risk that thinking itself suffers as a thinker becomes institutionalized; Deleuze would be the first to acknowledge as much. Deleuze, as During points out, was not very comfortable with being identified with a specific label and as 'a provider of theory'.[8] Still, Kaufman notes 'a striking imperative that circulates among those who read Deleuze: a drive to fidelity, or more nearly to not betray the master's thought, the trap that so many who write in his wake purportedly fall into.'[9] Kaufman also shows that while this 'drive to fidelity' exists in relation to many prominent thinkers, Deleuze's work posits particular difficulties in this respect. Because his work revolves so clearly around the importance of creative engagement – of approaching authors from behind – there is something almost inevitably paradoxical about coming after Deleuze in the sense that in order to be faithful, we must not be faithful. Deleuze's philosophy makes a lot more sense when read through active engagements that rely neither on the exegetical nor on applying his work to other texts – the two modes of engaging with Deleuzian thinking that Kaufman identifies as most common.[10] Rather, the most productive work is that which puts Deleuze to work beyond himself.

At the same time, however, and if being too faithful is to betray Deleuze's philosophy in the wrong way, it has become evident that the pendulum also strikes to its opposite, where the betrayal instead consists of taking the ball and running too far with it in the name of creativity. It is 'all too easy', as During writes, 'for commentators to rely on certain Deleuzian refrains – theory is a toolbox, concepts are bricks – in order to justify their own free treatment of Deleuze.'[11] At its extreme, such uses involve little engagement with his work and how it actually functions. Many of his concepts have also, During notes, become 'buzzwords, formulae, models', as they lend themselves nicely and sometimes a bit too easily to all sorts of things, to the point of becoming 'prepackaged slogans'. Both in and outside the scholarly world, concepts such as 'rhizome', 'smooth space' and 'war machine' are easily appropriated into a sort of 'pop philosophy'.[12] Reviewing books on Deleuze by Slavoj Žižek and Badiou, both of whom are well-established philosophers in their own right and both of whom have engaged with Deleuze's work in a rather critical fashion, Kaufman shows how they both call for a more productive betrayal than that of Deleuzian disciples who betray his work by following it too blindly,[13] and yet, they too in different ways struggle to find the balance. In fact, as Smith argues, both Badiou and Žižek build their critiques on a 'strategy of avoidance and displacement' that systematically avoids engaging with the core of the critique they offer.[14] It really is an art, it seems, the art of 'betraying well'.

Some of the most productive betrayals of Deleuze's work can be found in feminist and gender research that has increasingly discovered the usefulness of his philosophy. I noted earlier how the early feminist reception of Deleuze was sceptical. To a feminist movement to which the struggle for the specificity of a female subject position was central, Deleuzian ideas that insist on moving beyond such molar politics became problematic. To third-wave feminism, however, and to theories of sexuality and intersectionality that move away from the norms of identity politics, Deleuze's philosophy makes more sense. Here, we find an active mode of engagement which, obviously not exclusive to feminist or gender research, shows how we can continue to approach Deleuze 'from behind', although we might need to think of a less phallocentric figure for this kind of 'buggery'. Perhaps this mode of faithful infidelity, or faithless fidelity, can be traced back to the ambivalent attitudes that have characterized feminist approaches to Deleuze from the very beginning. The early feminist engagements with Deleuze recognized the dangers of taking on his work without care, as well as the productivity that comes with the risk. For example, in her book *Volatile Bodies: Toward a Corporeal Feminism* (1994), Grosz lists a number of pros and cons of engaging with Deleuze's work and comes to the conclusion that while 'it is important to tread warily on ground where one knows there are risks involved,' using his and Guattari's work with discernment may also take us places these philosophers 'may not go or even may not accept'.[15] In her *Nomadic Subjects: Embodiment and Sexual Difference in Contemporary Feminist Theory* from the same year, Braidotti critiques Deleuze even as she takes him on, suggesting that there is a 'genuine, positive contradiction' in his thinking that can be useful, even if 'Deleuze may well be the first one to demonstrate just how difficult it is to become consistently Deleuzian.'[16] And indeed, both Grosz and Braidotti have continued to use Deleuze in creative and experimental ways ever since then, and many have joined them.

Research on sex constitutes one related and telling example of a field in which Deleuze is taken beyond himself. Sex is quite usefully theorized from a Deleuzian perspective, even if he himself never developed this part of his philosophy to any great extent. While the liberation of desire functions to underscore its productivity and the politics of friendship serves to underline its dynamics, as we saw in Chapter Three, we can see also how it is not always easy for Deleuze to negotiate the combination of the impersonal and the embodied. This becomes particularly apparent when it comes to his understanding of sexuality. He suggests himself that there is in his work a relationship between sexuality and metaphysics 'that can be put into words' up until *The Logic of Sense*, but that after that comes to appear more 'like an ill-grounded abstraction'.[17] Still, the implications for sexuality of the non-Oedipal desire that Deleuze theorizes with Guattari are considerable. This conception of desire opens on to a critique of the domestication and gendering of sexuality that psychoanalysis tends to reinforce. Sexuality, Deleuze and Guattari insist, is not about two but about 'the production of a thousand sexes, which are so many uncontrollable becomings'.[18] So while there is great potential in this opening of sexuality, Deleuze did not explore this potential. However, this aspect of Deleuze and Guattari's work has been taken on and advanced by scholars who have come after them. 'Abstract sex', as a way of understanding sex not just beyond reproduction or discharge but beyond the body as a naturalized entity, sex beyond the human, as a way of recognizing the delimitations that humanistic categories have placed on our understanding of it, and 'sex after life', as a way of thinking sex as bound up with an understanding of life, are all examples of new theories of sexuality that have been inspired by Deleuze's work.[19]

Discourses on the post-, trans-, a- or in-human constitute another example of post-Deleuzian research that takes his work where he did not, could not or would not go. However, here it is worth noting that while some of this scholarship has been in a position to develop his work because it builds on scientific, political and theoretical developments that were not yet in place during his lifetime, much of this work also shows how Deleuze's work enables us to question categories of the human beyond their historical determination. Current discussions of the question of the human build on contrasting perspectives that, on the one hand, see the necessity to rethink the borders of the human as something that has occurred with the emergence of modern technologies and science, and on the other, regard the human as something that never really existed in the first place, at least not in the humanist sense. The latter perspective has much use of a Deleuzian philosophy that, in its very foundation, relies on theorizing life as a force beyond humanist categories. This can also be said to be the case in theories of 'new materialism' that, developed largely from the mid-1990s on by scholars such as Braidotti and Manuel DeLanda, resist a history of philosophy that has largely relied on a distinction between transcendent and materialist categories of being. Here, Deleuze's revitalization of thinkers such as Spinoza, Bergson and, more briefly, Alfred North Whitehead, is useful to projects interested in thinking about an embodied subjectivity that is not dualistically constructed.

Another important legacy of Deleuze has emerged in the sphere of political theory, a fact that becomes particularly interesting if compared with one that we noted earlier: that Deleuze was not as recognizably and actively political as many of his contemporaries. It is also within the realm of political thinking that much of the critique of Deleuze and the way his philosophy has been used has emerged in a post-Deleuzian context. Some, Smith notes, make a distinction between the 'good' Deleuze, which is the same as the solo Deleuze, and the 'bad' Deleuze, which is the work he conducted with Guattari. One 'can only regret', writes Žižek, 'that the Anglo-Saxon reception of Deleuze (and, also, the political impact of Deleuze) is predominantly that of a "guattarized" Deleuze.'[20] In the case of Žižek, Smith notes, the critique relies at least partly on the way he contrasts what he sees as a good reading of Lacan in the earlier *The Logic of Sense* with a bad one in *Anti-Oedipus*. But for Žižek as well as for Badiou and Derrida, this distinction between the good and the bad Deleuze is also made because Guattari is seen to have influenced Deleuze towards the political in an undesirable way.[21] Žižek suggests that Deleuze's attraction to Guattari was perhaps based on the need to attain an alibi for, or 'easy escape' from, an earlier position that generated work that was never directly political.[22] Once Žižek gathers steam, his critique intensifies and he ultimately questions the current use of Deleuze within the anti-global political left, suggesting that his work contains, however unintended, 'features that justify calling Deleuze the ideologist of late capitalism'.[23] Apart from Žižek's critique, other harsh and well-known critiques in the post-Deleuzian context come from Badiou and Peter Hallward, who suggest that his work is useless for real-world political engagement. Hallward, for example, argues that Deleuze's philosophy 'amounts to little more than utopian distraction' and that although many 'enthusiasts' engage with Deleuzian thought for political aims, it is 'essentially indifferent to the politics of this world'.[24]

But many have also pointed to the relevance of Deleuze precisely for the politics of this world. Hardt and Negri's well-known and much discussed work *Empire*, which was published in three volumes through the first decade of the new millennium, builds in part on Deleuze's work.[25] A central element here is Deleuze's theorization of the development of society from one that executes a disciplinary power by means of identities, institutions and moulds, to a 'society of control' in which power relies rather on open modulations of behaviours and desires. Deleuze builds on Foucault's theories on biopolitics but also diverges from and develops them.[26] This is one of the many instances in which Deleuzian theory seems to become more rather than less relevant as time goes by. The translation of Foucault's *The Birth of Biopolitics*, which contains the lectures that he gave on the topic at the Collège de France in 1978–9, into English in 2008 has been followed by the online publication of Deleuze's course lectures on Foucault that he, as we saw in the chapter on friendship, gave every week at University of Paris VIII in 1985–6. Transcripts of the latter were completed in 2013.[27] In other words, there is currently a rather active engagement with Deleuze's work from a political perspective.

Deleuze's work has proved useful also to those interested in finding productive ways of understanding and working with resistance and activism. For Deleuze, resistance must not model itself on the same terms as that which it resists but must invent new ways of being. As we have seen earlier, this can be traced back to a Nietzschean approach that recognizes reactive forces as bound only to negate or confirm what already is, and that thus emphasizes the importance of active forces as capable of creating something new. Because Deleuze's work centres on this insistence on the active, it enables a particular way of thinking about resistance that is not governed by the rules of that which it resists. Thus he has come to be repeatedly evoked to 'think the radical alternative', as Braidotti and Rick Dolphijn put it, to become 'a people that was missing' in a contemporary context in which it is hard to envision 'viable alternatives'.[28] Deleuze's work, Marcelo Svirsky argues, provides the conceptual tools to resist a 'royal science of politics' that claims political effort into its dominant discourse, and enables us to think innovatively about activism.[29] With the help of Deleuzian thinking, Svirsky suggests, we can make space for 'activist experiences that refuse simply to align with "the given" of formal politics'.[30] Examples of the dynamics of the tensions between activist and formal politics can be seen in the ways organizations such as Wikileaks or animal rights movements work to create ruptures in the way we think and work, at the same time as they are threatened by appropriation by a royal science that will make them conform to majoritarian political structures: 'After Deleuze and Guattari, political activism may be approached in a fundamentally different way: without an image, without a form.'[31] As Deleuze and Parnet write: 'why not think that *a new type of revolution is in the course of becoming possible?*'[32]

But we can also find examples of ways in which the relevance of Deleuzian thought for political aims has been recognized by projects with which he himself profoundly disagreed. We noted in Chapter Three how he was engaged with and deeply critical of the Israeli occupation of Palestinian territory and we can therefore make an informed guess of how he would have reacted to the fact that the Israeli Defense Forces (IDF) have read and been inspired by his and Guattari's theories of space, territoriality and rhizomes for their military operations: 'Several of the concepts in *A Thousand Plateaus*', former Israeli general Shimon Naveh describes, 'became instrumental for us . . . allowing us to explain contemporary situations in a way that we could not have otherwise explained . . . We try to produce the operational space in such a manner that borders do not affect us.'[33] In lectures, Naveh has also referred directly to Deleuze and Guattari's work on the war machine: 'it is a matter of deterritorializing the enemy by shattering his territory from within.'[34] From this rises a highly relevant question, one that Eyal Weizman tries to explore – that is, 'what is at stake in the uses of such theoretical "tools" by military thinkers, especially since they are the very same tools through which forms of oppositional critique have themselves frequently been articulated?'[35] And indeed, Deleuze's work has been used on both sides of the wall, as Deleuze scholars have given a series of lectures at the International Academy of Art in the Palestinian Ramallah.

Graffiti of Deleuze at the Abode of Chaos, Saint-Roman-au-Mont-d'Or, France.

Guattari, commenting on Foucault's oft-repeated statement that this century will one day be Deleuzian, hoped that it would be so not because it would be connected with Deleuze's thought but because it would 'comprise a certain reassemblage of theoretical activity vis-à-vis university institutions and power institutions of all kinds.'[36] The century that Foucault refers to is, of course, the century that we have now left behind, but although we have not yet seen much of the century that has come after it, it seems as though theories of the changing nature of university and power institutions will be much needed, and that Deleuze's now already several-decades-old work is becoming an increasingly useful tool. Deleuze himself, commenting on Foucault's statement, said that he did not know what Foucault might have meant, but suggested that he might have been referring to a rather poignant difference between himself and the others of their generation. Unlike most others, Deleuze notes,

> I haven't approached things through structure, or linguistics or psychoanalysis, through science or even through history, because I think philosophy has its own raw material that allows it to enter into more fundamental external relations with these other disciplines. Maybe that's what Foucault meant: I wasn't better than the others, but more naïve, producing a kind of *art brut*, so to speak; not the most profound but the most innocent.[37]

And perhaps there is a certain innocence to Deleuze's philosophy. His insistence on the creative force of life does not seem to rhyme well with the increasingly frequent wake-up calls when it comes to looming threats such as climate change, global surveillance and aggressive fundamentalism in the new millennium. But perhaps we also need a certain amount of innocence to persevere through the cumulative sense of hopelessness and cynicism that such threats and our inadequate ability to deal with them keep generating. Deleuze, as Rajchman reminds us, emphasizes the need to believe 'beyond the assurance of knowledge, or faith' – this would be a true 'belief in the world'. Because 'to "affirm life" is never to affirm a proposition or thesis about life, but on the contrary, to engage in another non-assertional style of thinking – to affirm is then to disburden or "lighten", to attain the "innocence" of other possibilities.'[38] If there is one Deleuzian legacy that we may need more than ever today, it is, perhaps, the potential of such a sharp and well-informed innocence; the insistence on other possibilities.

References

Prologue

1 Gilles Deleuze and Claire Parnet, *Dialogues II*, trans. Hugh Tomlinson and Barbara Habberjam (New York, 2007), p. 5.

2 Hannah Arendt, 'Heidegger at Eighty', in *Heidegger and Modern Philosophy: Critical Essays*, ed. Michael Murray (New Haven, CT, and London, 1978), p. 303. Arendt's essay was originally published in the *New York Review of Books* in 1971.

3 Friedrich Nietzsche, *Beyond Good and Evil: On the Genealogy of Morality*, trans. Adrian Del Caro (Stanford, CA, 2014), p. 9.

4 Jacques Derrida cited in Benoît Peeters, *Derrida: A Biography*, trans. Andrew Brown (Cambridge, 2013), p. 2.

5 Roland Barthes, 'The Death of the Author', in Barthes, *Image – Music – Text*, trans. and ed. Stephen Heath (London, 1977), p. 147. See also Michel Foucault, 'What is an Author?', in *Aesthetics, Method, and Epistemology*, ed. James D. Faubion, trans. Robert Hurley et al. (New York, 1998).

6 Peter Osborne, 'Guattareuze?', *New Left Review*, 69 (2011), p. 139.

7 Gilles Deleuze, *Lettres et autres textes*, ed. David Lapoujade (Paris, 2015), p. 52: 'on préfère vous gommer, et moi, m'abstractifier'. The letters in this collection have not been translated into English and therefore all the translations from this volume are my own. I would also like to take this opportunity to acknowledge the much needed assistance of Sarah Bouttier when it comes to these translations. To ensure transparency and also provide a sense of Deleuze's own language, I will, in the cases of direct quotation, continue to give the French in the references. Another example of how Deleuze was aware

that Guattari ended up in his shadow can be found in Deleuze's letters to Arnaud Villani, which, stretching across several years while Villani was working on a book on Deleuze, also show how the latter repeatedly and with increasing impatience had to insist that Guattari not be excluded in discussions of their joint work. (See *Lettres et autres textes*, pp. 82, 85, 86.)

8   Osborne, 'Guattareuze?', p. 141.

9   I have tried, however, to be careful in my reliance on Dosse's biography since errors have been identified both in his original text and as a result of the translation into English. See Alan D. Schrift, 'Intersecting Lives', *Symploke*, xx/1–2 (2012), pp. 3–4. While referring mostly to the English translation, I have checked it against the French original. Here I would like to acknowledge the generous assistance of Hanta Persson. In the case of direct quotation from the translation, I have also provided the French original in the accompanying reference.

10 This second difference places my study in a somewhat uneasy, if hopefully productive, tension with Dosse's. On the one hand, I, like many reviewers, miss a critical and reflexive engagement in Dosse's study. Evgeni V. Pavlov, for example, argues that Dosse's 'explicit *non*-engagement with the rich philosophical material under consideration is consistent to the point of being programmatic.' See Evgeni V. Pavlov, 'The Banality of Genius: When Deleuze Met Guattari', *Parallax*, xviii/1 (2012), pp. 112–16. See also Osborne, 'Guattareuze?'. On the other hand, I also agree with those who find it an important and impressive contribution to the field. Thomas Nail, for example, calls it 'an indispensible resource' (Thomas Nail, 'Review', *Foucault Studies*, xiv (2012), pp. 218–22). Ultimately, I am most grateful for what some have called the overwhelming thoroughness of his extensive chronicle and am indebted to it as it has enabled me to single out reverberant events and accounts and situate them within a different kind of critical framework.

11 Initially, I considered several different ways of structuring this biography. A first idea was to work with series (*series*). Deleuze uses this method in *Logique de sens* (*The Logic of Sense*) to try to get beyond the problem of representation. While representation delimits the difference and the multiplicities inherent in all things by assuming them under modes of resemblance and identity, the series opens a

way of bringing them out. It works, essentially, by running pairs of series in parallel – so for example a series of events and a series of states of things – allowing them to connect in unexpected ways and thereby to unsettle the most obvious constructions of identity and representation. A second idea was to employ plateaus (*plateaux*) as do Deleuze and Guattari in *A Thousand Plateaus*. A plateau is a bringing together of disparate intensities and concepts from different contexts to build temporary but dynamic states. Rather than closing thinking down by following predetermined routes and structures, the plateau is a way of allowing otherwise hidden intensities to emerge.

12 Gilles Deleuze and Félix Guattari, *Kafka: Toward a Minor Literature*, trans. Dana Polan (Minneapolis, MN, 1986), p. 81.

13 Ibid., pp. 83–4.

14 Gilles Deleuze, *Negotiations*, trans. Martin Joughin (New York, 1995), p. 7.

15 Jacques Rancière, 'Is There a Deleuzian Aesthetics?', trans. Radmila Djordjevic, *Qui Parle*, XIV/2 (2004), p. 1.

16 Eleanor Kaufman, 'Betraying Well', *Criticism*, XLIV/4 (2004), pp. 651–9.

1 A Child

1 Gilles Deleuze and Claire Parnet, *L'Abécédaire de Gilles Deleuze*, dir. Pierre-André Boutang (Video Editions Montparnasse, 1988–9), 'E comme enfance'. Translated by Charles J. Stivale as *Gilles Deleuze from A to Z* (Cambridge and New York, 2012), 'E as in Enfance'.

2 Deleuze and Parnet, *Gilles Deleuze from A to Z*, 'E as in Enfance'. Stivale's translations are used throughout this study.

3 François Dosse, *Gilles Deleuze and Félix Guattari: Intersecting Lives*, trans. Deborah Glassman (New York, 2010), p. 88.

4 Anna Catherine Hickey-Moody, 'Deleuze's Children', *Educational Philosophy and Theory*, XLV/3 (2013), p. 272.

5 In the constant flux that is life, certain entities become more permanent than others. Thus, for example, a person is a molar construct insofar as we perceive of and respond to them as a unity. Molar constructs can be very helpful as they provide tools for interaction – it is, no doubt, pretty convenient to be able to refer

to a person, a gender, a nationality without always accounting for those dimensions that problematize such constructs – but they are also highly susceptible to a disabling politics. If we look at a helpful description of the molar and its logic provided by Brian Massumi, we can immediately see this ambivalence: 'A molarized individual is a "person" to the extent that a category (cultural image of unity) has been imposed on it and insofar as its subsequent actions are made to conform to those prescribed by its assigned category.' Brian Massumi, *A User's Guide to Capitalism and Schizophrenia: Deviations from Deleuze and Guattari* (Cambridge, MA, and London, 1992), p. 55. In other words, the molar sets up boundaries that simultaneously help and obstruct life. An example can be taken from the different waves of feminism. Where a second-wave feminism fought to ascertain a specificity of the category of 'woman', the third wave saw that, as our 'subsequent actions are made to conform to those prescribed by its assigned category', it was also a delimiting, molar construct that disregarded and even disabled other modes of being.

6   Deleuze, in *Gilles Deleuze from A to Z*, 'E as in Enfance'.
7   Ibid.
8   Daniel W. Smith, 'Introduction, "A Life of Pure Immanence"': Deleuze's "Critique et Clinique" Project', in Gilles Deleuze, *Essays Critical and Clinical*, trans. Daniel W. Smith and Michael A. Greco (Minneapolis, MN, 1997), p. xi.
9   Deleuze, in *Gilles Deleuze from A to Z*, 'E as in Enfance'.
10 Michel Tournier, *The Wind Spirit: An Autobiography*, trans. Arthur Goldhammer (London, 1989), pp. 127–8.
11 Ibid., p. 128.
12 Dosse, *Gilles Deleuze and Félix Guattari*, pp. 90–92.
13 Daniel W. Smith, 'Gilles Deleuze', in *Poststructuralism and Critical Theory's Second Generation*, ed. Alan D. Schrift (London and New York, 2014), p. 93.
14 Gilles Deleuze, *Negotiations*, trans. Martin Joughin (New York, 1995), p. 5.
15 Tournier, *The Wind Spirit*, p. 128.
16 Smith, 'Gilles Deleuze', p. 92.
17 Tournier, *The Wind Spirit*, p. 131.
18 Gilles Deleuze, *Desert Islands and Other Texts, 1953–1974*, ed. David Lapoujade, trans. Michael Taormina (New York, 2004), p. 77.

19 Ibid.

20 Originally published in *Poésie* as 'Description de la femme. Pour une philosophie d'autrui sexuée', *Poésie*, XLV/28 (October–November 1945), pp. 28–39.

21 Christian Kerslake, *Deleuze and the Unconscious* (London and New York, 2007), p. 1.

22 Ibid.

23 Joshua Ramey, *The Hermetic Deleuze: Philosophy and the Spiritual Ordeal* (Durham, NC, 2012), pp. 89–90.

24 Some of this material is now available in a special issue of the journal *Collapse – Collapse*, III: *Unknown Deleuze [+Speculative Realism]*, ed. Robin Mackay (2012).

25 Kerslake, *Deleuze and the Unconscious*, p. 125.

26 Ramey, *The Hermetic Deleuze*, p. 103.

27 Joshua Delpech-Ramey, 'Deleuze, Guattari, and the "Politics of Sorcery"', *SubStance*, XXXIX/1 (2010), p. 17.

28 Kerslake, *Deleuze and the Unconscious*, p. 70.

29 Ibid., pp. 69, 74; for Deleuze's early essay on masochism, see 'De Sacher-Masoch au masochisme', *Arguments*, 21 (1961).

30 Gilles Deleuze, *Cinema II: The Time-image*, trans. Hugh Tomlinson and Robert Galeta (Minneapolis, MN, 1989), p. 98.

31 Ibid., pp. 98–9.

32 Gilles Deleuze and Clare Parnet, *Dialogues II*, trans. Hugh Tomlinson and Barbara Habberjam (New York, 2007), p. 65.

33 I am referring here to Baudrillard's 'Forget Foucault', an essay submitted to *Critique*, a French journal on whose editorial board Foucault himself served. The essay contained a heavy critique of Foucault as well as others who believed in revolutionary desire, such as Deleuze. The essay was subsequently published in book form: Jean Baudrillard, *Forget Foucault*, trans. Nicole Dufresne, Phil Beitchman, Lee Hildreth and Mark Polizzotri (New York, 1987).

34 Friedrich Nietzsche, *On the Genealogy of Morals and Ecce Homo*, ed. Walter Kaufman, trans. Walter Kaufman and R. J. Hollingdale (New York, 1989), pp. 57–8.

35 Deleuze and Parnet, *Dialogues II*, p. 78.

36 Friedrich Nietzsche, *Thus Spoke Zarathustra*, trans. Thomas Common (Raleigh, NC, 1999, ebook), 'I. The Three Metamorphoses'.

2 An Apprenticeship

1   Gilles Deleuze, *Negotiations*, trans. Martin Joughin (New York, 1995), p. 6.
2   In France, the *Agrégation de philosophie* is an annual exam that rewards a certificate to teach philosophy in secondary and post-secondary school. The exam is usually taken after completing one's studies at university or a *grande école*.
3   Giuseppe Bianco, *Après Bergson: Portrait de groupe avec philosophe* (Paris, 2015), p. 286.
4   Ibid., p. 288.
5   Deleuze, *Negotiations*, p. 5.
6   Gilles Deleuze and Claire Parnet, *Dialogues II*, trans. Hugh Tomlinson and Barbara Habberjam (New York, 2007), p. 13.
7   Alan D. Schrift, email exchange with the author.
8   These books are *Nietzsche et la philosophie* (1962) [*Nietzsche and Philosophy*, 1983], *La Philosophie critique de Kant* (1963) [*The Critical Philosophy of Kant*, 1984], *Le Bergsonisme* (1966) [*Bergsonism*, 1988], *Spinoza et le problème de l'expression* (1968) [*Expressionism in Philosophy: Spinoza*, 1990] and later also *Spinoza: Philosophie pratique* (1970, new edn 1981) [*Spinoza: Practical Philosophy*, 1988], *Foucault* (1986) [*Foucault*, 1988] and *Le Pli: Leibniz et le Baroque* (1988) [*The Fold: Leibniz and the Baroque*, 1993].
9   François Dosse, *Gilles Deleuze and Félix Guattari: Intersecting Lives*, trans. Deborah Glassman (New York, 2010), p. 110.
10 Alan D. Schrift, 'The Effects on the *Agrégation de Philosophie* on Twentieth-century French Philosophy', *Journal of the History of Philosophy*, XLVI/3 (2008), p. 467.
11 For a more detailed account of how this list functions, see Schrift, 'The Effects on the *Agrégation de Philosophie*', pp. 449–73.
12 Gilles Deleuze and Claire Parnet, *L'Abécédaire de Gilles Deleuze*, dir. Pierre-André Boutang (Video Editions Montparnasse, 1988–9), 'H comme histoire de la philosophie'. Translated by Charles J. Stivale as *Gilles Deleuze From A to Z* (Cambridge and New York, 2012), 'H as in History of Philosophy'.
13 Daniel W. Smith, 'Gilles Deleuze', in *Poststructuralism and Critical Theory's Second Generation*, ed. Alan D. Schrift (London and New York, 2014), p. 91.

14 Ibid., p. 93.
15 Deleuze, *Negotiations*, p. 6.
16 Dosse, *Gilles Deleuze and Félix Guattari*, p. 109.
17 Michel Serres, cited in Smith, 'Gilles Deleuze', p. 92.
18 Deleuze, *Negotiations*, p. 122.
19 Alan D. Schrift, 'French Nietzscheanism', in *Poststructuralism and Critical Theory's Second Generation*, p. 39.
20 Deleuze and Parnet, *Dialogues II*, p. 14.
21 Deleuze, *Negotiations*, p. 125.
22 Ibid., p. 84.
23 The reason why Deleuze's dissertations were published before his defence was that the defence, originally planned for the autumn of 1968, had to be postponed because of his illness. I expand on this further in Chapter Five.
24 Bianco, *Après Bergson*, pp. 291–2. This book offers a thorough account of the importance of Bergson to Deleuze's philosophy.
25 Published in English as 'Bergson's Conception of Difference', in *Desert Islands and Other Texts, 1953–1974*, ed. David Lapoujade, trans. Michael Taormina (Paris, 2004).
26 Gilles Deleuze, *Difference and Repetition*, trans. Paul Patton (London and New York, 2004), p. 330.
27 Deleuze, *Negotiations*, pp. 60–61.
28 Deleuze, *Difference and Repetition*, p. 366.
29 Deleuze, *Negotiations*, p. 125.
30 Ibid., p. 138.
31 Deleuze and Parnet, *Dialogues II*, p. 10.
32 See *Essays Critical and Clinical*, trans. Daniel W. Smith and Michael A. Greco (Minneapolis, MN, 1997), p. 188 n. 1.
33 In Deleuze and Parnet, *Dialogues II*, pp. 10, 109.
34 Félix Guattari, *The Anti-Oedipus Papers*, ed. Stéphane Nadaud, trans. Kélina Gotman (New York, 2006), p. 308. Other examples that speak to Fanny's influence include 'In principle I don't write stuff like this, except if it comes to my pen onto paper of its own accord. I just kept myself from writing "through the course of my pen" ["au flu de la plume"] because I think I remember that that's just the kind of expression that annoys Fanny' (p. 354).
35 Deleuze and Parnet, *Dialogues II*, p. 18.

36 Deleuze, *Negotiations*, p. 10.

37 Guattari writes down dreams in which Fanny dies, allowing for greater closeness between him and Deleuze and room for Guattari to help out with the children (p. 322), and of Fanny rejecting his writing as useless (p. 353). 'So is it necessary', he asks himself, 'to see in this fantasy of Fanny's death the vengeful correlate to an exclusive homosexual choice with respect to Gilles? Service theory would make me admit: you wanted to kill the mother-wife for love of the father-husband. But that's not how I feel!' (p. 322). He tries to exclude her at one point, which seems to immediately also create a distance to Deleuze – 'It's the first time I write Deleuze here instead of Gilles. No more Fanny. Epiphany. A cavity of lack' – only to, a few lines down, give in and take them both back: 'I will keep giving these texts to Fanny and, at the end of the chain, Gilles' (p. 400). All page references are to Guattari, *The Anti-Oedipus Papers.*

38 Deleuze and Parnet, *Dialogues II*, p. 35.

39 Schrift, 'French Nietzscheanism', pp. 24–5.

40 As David Lapoujade notes, there are also additional writings – those written before 1953 and previously unpublished or posthumous texts – but which are not included, respecting Deleuze's conditions for publication. See David Lapoujade, 'Introduction', in Gilles Deleuze, *Desert Islands and Other Texts, 1953–1974*, ed. David Lapoujade, trans. Michael Taormina (New York, 2004).

41 Dosse, *Gilles Deleuze and Félix Guattari*, pp. 116–17. 'Il avait réponse à tout et avec des renversements suprenants'; François Dosse, *Gilles Deleuze et Félix Guattari: Biographie Croisée* (Paris, 2007), p. 145.

42 Alain Badiou, *Deleuze: The Clamor of Being*, trans. Louise Burchill (Minneapolis, MN, 2000), p. 1.

43 Michael Hardt, *Gilles Deleuze: An Apprenticeship in Philosophy* (Minneapolis, MN, 1993), pp. xx–xxi.

44 Véronique Bergen, 'Deleuze and the Question of Ontology', in *Gilles Deleuze: The Intensive Reduction*, ed. Constantin V. Boundas (London and New York, 2009), pp. 7–22.

46 'S'ils n'ont pas été mangés'. Gilles Deleuze, *Lettres et autres textes*, ed. David Lapoujade (Paris, 2015), p. 34.

47 Dosse, *Gilles Deleuze and Félix Guattari*, p. 177.

48 Deleuze in *L'Abécédaire*, 'G as in Gauche'.

49 Charles J. Stivale, *Gilles Deleuze's ABCs: The Folds of Friendship* (Baltimore, MD, 2008), p. 6.

50 'Mon orgueil en ressort cuisant'. Deleuze, *Lettres et autres textes*, p. 59.

51 Dosse, *Gilles Deleuze and Félix Guattari*, p. 347.

52 Hugh Tomlinson and Barbara Haberjam, 'Translators' Introduction', in Deleuze and Parnet, *Dialogues II*, pp. xi–xii.

53 Badiou, *Deleuze: The Clamor of Being*, p. 2.

54 For a more detailed account of these conflicts and events, see Dosse, *Gilles Deleuze and Félix Guattari*, pp. 347–50.

55 Ibid., p. 350.

3 A Friendship

1 Gilles Deleuze and Claire Parnet, *Dialogues II*, trans. Hugh Tomlinson and Barbara Habberjam (New York, 2007), p. 17.

2 Alain Badiou, *Deleuze: The Clamor of Being*, trans. Louise Burchill (Minneapolis, MN, 2000), p. 1. For a detailed account of some of the philosophical disagreements and tensions between Deleuze and Badiou, see Giuseppe Bianco, *Après Bergson: Portrait de groupe avec philosophe* (Paris, 2015).

3 Gilles Deleuze, *Lettres et autres textes*, ed. David Lapoujade (Paris, 2015), pp. 24–5, my translation.

4 Charles J. Stivale, *Gilles Deleuze's ABC: The Folds of Friendship* (Baltimore, MD, 2008), p. xiii.

5 See ibid.

6 Gilles Deleuze and Claire Parnet, *L'Abécédaire de Gilles Deleuze*, dir. Pierre-André Boutang (Video Editions Montparnasse, 1989–9), 'F comme fidélité'. Translated by Charles J. Stivale as *Gilles Deleuze from A to Z* (Cambridge and New York, 2012), 'F for Fidelity'.

7 Gilles Deleuze, *Proust and Signs: The Complete Text*, trans. Richard Howard (London and New York, 2008), pp. 60–61. In the work of Proust, Deleuze finds a critique of such friendship, which is also, then, a critique of philosophy, as it creates encounters with signs beyond goodwill. Via Proust, he finds that friendship based on 'well-disposed minds that are explicitly in agreement as to the signification of things, words, and ideas' are about as useful to

philosophy as is the philosopher who 'presupposes in himself the benevolence of thought, who attributes to thought the natural love of truth and to truth the explicit determination of what is naturally worked out by thought' (p. 20).

8   Stivale, *Gilles Deleuze's ABC*, p. 3. Deleuze's understanding of friendship was also influenced by his lifetime friend Maurice de Gandillac, as Stivale shows, p. 12.

9   Ibid., pp. 1–2.

10 Gilles Deleuze, *The Fold: Leibniz and the Baroque*, trans. Tom Conley (Minneapolis, MN, 1993), p. 19.

11 Gilles Deleuze and Félix Guattari, *What is Philosophy?*, trans. Graham Burchell and Hugh Tomlinson (London, 1994), p. 3.

12 'En fait, il y a seulement rhizome entre Félix et moi.' Deleuze, *Lettres et autres textes*, p. 78.

13 Ibid., pp. 35–6.

14 Ibid., pp. 40–44.

15 'Pourquoi êtes-vous amené à donner un privilège apparent à l'expression du point de vue de l'agencement? Il faudrait que vous m'expliquiez avec patience'. Deleuze, *Lettres et autres textes*, p. 55.

16 Gilles Deleuze, 'Letter to Uno: How Félix and I Worked Together', in Deleuze, *Two Regimes of Madness: Texts and Interviews, 1975–1995*, ed. David Lapoujade, trans. Ames Hodges and Mike Taormina (New York, 2007), pp. 238–9.

17 François Dosse, *Gilles Deleuze and Félix Guattari: Intersecting Lives*, trans. Deborah Glassman (New York, 2010), p. 7.

18 'Vous êtes un prodigieux inventeur de concepts <<sauvages>>', Deleuze, *Lettres et autres textes*, p. 56.

19 In Dosse, *Gilles Deleuze and Félix Guattari*, p. 8. Guattari: 'Cette collaboration n'est pas le résultat d'une simple rencontre entre deux individus. Outre le concours de circonstances, c'est aussi tout un contexte politique qui nous y a conduits. Il s'est agi, à l'origine, moins de la mise en commun d'un savoir que de cumul de nos incertitudes, et même d'un certain désarroi devant la tournure qu'avaient prise les événements après Mai 68.' Deleuze: 'Si nous avons essayé de dépasser cette dualité traditionnelle, c'est précisément parce que nous écrivions à deux. Aucun de nous n'était le fou, aucun le psychiatre, il fallait être deux pour dégager un

processus . . . Le processus, c'est ce que nous appelons le flux.'
(François Dosse, *Gilles Deleuze et Félix Guattari: Biographie Croisée*
(Paris, 2007), p. 19).

20 Gilles Deleuze, 'Letter to Uno on Language', in Deleuze, *Two Regimes of Madness*, p. 201.

21 Deleuze, 'Preface to the American Edition of *Dialogues II*', in Deleuze, *Two Regimes of Madness*, p. 311.

22 Félix Guattari, *The Anti-Oedipus Papers*, ed. Stéphane Nadaud, trans. Kélina Gotman (New York, 2006), p. 399.

23 Ibid., p. 400.

24 Dosse, *Gilles Deleuze and Félix Guattari*, p. 13.

25 Deleuze, 'Letter to Uno: How Félix and I Worked Together', p. 239.

26 Stivale, *Gilles Deleuze's ABCs*, p. 10.

27 Deleuze, 'Letter to Uno: How Félix and I Worked Together', p. 240.

28 'Et là le centre serait pour moi la recherche d'une réponse toute claire et simple à Qu'est-ce que la philosophie?' Deleuze, *Lettres et autres textes*, p. 55.

29 In Dosse, *Gilles Deleuze and Félix Guattari*, p. 4. 'D'avoir à vous recontrer quand cela vous sera possible constitue pour moi un événement déjà présent rétroactivement à partir de plusieurs origines' (Dosse, *Biographie croisée*, p. 15).

30 'Moi aussi, sens que nous sommes amis avant de nous connaître'. Deleuze, *Lettres et autres textes*, p. 35.

31 See Dosse, *Gilles Deleuze and Félix Guattari*, pp. 6 ('they never became profoundly close') and 16 ('All of their close friends were aware of the intensity of this friendship.' 'I have rarely seen two people truly love and value each other as much as Gilles and Félix') respectively.

32 This is an expression that does not translate very easily into English; approximately 'I embrace you strongly.' Deleuze, *Lettres et autres textes*, p. 54.

33 Guattari, cited in Stéphane Nadaud, 'Love Story between an Orchid and a Wasp', in Guattari, *The Anti-Oedipus Papers*, p. 14.

34 Cited in Stivale, *Gilles Deleuze's ABCs*, p. 132.

35 Guattari, *The Anti-Oedipus Papers*, p. 323.

36 Deleuze, *Negotiations*, p. 7.

37 Ibid.

38 Stivale, *Gilles Deleuze's ABCs*, p. 135.

39 'Vos notes encore sont extrêmement belles et moi, je suis de plus en plus lent.' Deleuze, *Lettres et autres textes*, p. 46.

40 Deleuze, 'Letter to Uno: How Félix and I Worked Together', p. 237.

41 Deleuze and Parnet, *Dialogues II*, p. 16.

42 Gilles Deleuze, 'For Félix', in *Two Regimes of Madness*, p. 387.

43 Deleuze, *Negotiations*, p. 83.

44 Ibid.

45 John Marks, *Gilles Deleuze: Vitalism and Multiplicity* (London, 1998), pp. 108–9.

46 Ibid., p. 109. See also Michel Foucault and Gilles Deleuze, 'Intellectuals and Power: A Conversation between Michel Foucault and Gilles Deleuze', reprinted in Foucault, *Language, Counter-memory, Practice: Selected Essays and Interviews*, ed. Donald F. Bouchard (New York, 1977), pp. 205–17.

47 Dosse, *Gilles Deleuze and Félix Guattari*, pp. 310–12.

48 Eleanor Kaufman, *The Delirium of Praise: Bataille, Blanchot, Deleuze, Foucault, Klossowski* (Baltimore, MD, 2001), p. 80.

49 Kaufman's entire study, *The Delirium of Praise*, is devoted to analysing such exchanges. The other names she looks specifically at are Georges Bataille, Blanchot and Klossowski.

50 Deleuze, *Negotiations*, p. 107.

51 Deleuze, *Lettres et autres textes*, p. 68.

52 'À la fois j'ai l'impression que vous me comprenez pleinement, et que en meme temps vous me dépassez. C'est donc le rêve.' Deleuze, *Lettres et autres textes*, p. 68.

53 Deleuze, *Negotiations*, p. 102.

54 Cited in Stivale, *Gilles Deleuze's ABCs*, p. 71.

55 Michel Foucault, 'Theatrum Philosophicum', in *Language, Counter-memory, Practice*, pp. 165–96.

56 Marks, *Gilles Deleuze*, p. 79.

57 Deleuze, *Negotiations*, p. 4.

58 Kaufman, *The Delirium of Praise*, p. 122.

59 Marks, *Gilles Deleuze*, p. 110.

60 Dosse, *Gilles Deleuze and Félix Guattari*, p. 315.

61 'Tout est bien noir, et l'histoire du Liban m'a paru insupportable.' Deleuze, *Lettres et autres textes*, p. 56.

62 All four texts are republished in Deleuze, *Two Regimes of Madness*.

63 Deleuze, 'The Importance of Being Arafat', in *Two Regimes of Madness*, pp. 242, 244.

64 'Don't be ridiculous', he says in response to the question of whether his rejection of the Nouveaux Philosophes is a reaction to their attack on him and Guattari. Deleuze, 'On the New Philosophers (Plus a More General Problem)', in *Two Regimes of Madness*, p. 139.

65 Gregory Flaxman, *Gilles Deleuze and the Fabulation of Philosophy* (Minneapolis, MN, 2012), pp. 249–50.

66 Deleuze, 'On the New Philosophers', p. 147.

67 Ibid., p. 139.

68 'Ma petite force, c'est de n'avoir jamais répondu à rien ni participé à une polémique.' Deleuze, *Lettres et autres textes*, p. 242.

69 Deleuze, 'On the New Philosophers', p. 140.

70 Flaxman, *Gilles Deleuze and the Fabulation of Philosophy*, p. 253.

71 In an interview with Dosse, Deleuze's friend Jacques Donzelot recalls Deleuze's words as follows: 'Jacques, what do you think, Michel is completely nuts, what's this old idea about truth? He's taking us back to that old idea, veridiction! Oh, it can't be!' Dosse, *Gilles Deleuze and Félix Guattari*, p. 318.

72 François Ewald, 'Editorial Foreword', in Gilles Deleuze, 'Desire and Pleasure', trans. Melissa McMahon (1997), www.artdes.monash.edu.au/globe/delfou.html#1, accessed 25 November 2016. Translation of Deleuze, 'Désir et plaisir', *Magazine littéraire*, 325 (October 1994), pp. 59–65.

73 Deleuze, 'Desire and Pleasure', in *Two Regimes*, p. 133.

74 Ewald, 'Editorial Foreword', n.p..

75 For a more in depth analysis of the differences between Deleuze and Foucault on the notion of sexuality, see Frida Beckman, *Between Desire and Pleasure: A Deleuzian Theory of Sexuality* (Edinburgh, 2013).

76 Ewald, 'Editorial Foreword', n.p..

77 Dosse, *Biographie croisée*, p. 328.

78 Deleuze, *Negotiations*, p. 94.

79 Stivale, *Gilles Deleuze's ABCs*, p. 72.

80 Deleuze, *Negotiations*, pp. 85–6.

81 Deleuze and Parnet, *Dialogues II*, p. 11.

82 Gilles Deleuze, *Foucault*, trans. Seán Hand (London and New York, 2006), pp. 79–88.

83 Deleuze, *Negotiations*, p. 98.

84 Gilles Deleuze, 'May '68 Did Not Take Place', in *Two Regimes of Madness*, pp. 233–6.

85 Paul Patton, 'Introduction', *Deleuze and the Political* (London, 2000), p. 1. As Patton's edited collection *Deleuze and the Political* shows, however, there are many ways of reading and understanding Deleuze politically.

86 Ian Buchanan and Nicholas Thoburn, 'Introduction: Deleuze and Politics', in *Deleuze and Politics*, ed. Paul Patton (Edinburgh, 2008), pp. 3–4.

87 Ibid., p. 1.

88 Gregg Lambert, *Who's Afraid of Deleuze and Guattari?* (London and New York, 2006), p. 4.

89 Michel Foucault, 'Preface', in Gilles Deleuze and Félix Guattari, *Anti-Oedipus: Capitalism and Schizophrenia*, trans. Robert Hurley, Mark Seem and Helen R. Lane (Minneapolis, MN, 2005), p. xiv.

90 Stivale, *Gilles Deleuze's ABCs*, pp. xiv–xv.

91 Schrift, in email exchange with the author, May 2016.

92 Stivale, *Gilles Deleuze's ABCs*, p. 92.

93 Ibid., p. 96.

94 Ibid., p. 84.

95 Kaufman, *The Delirium of Praise*, p. 7.

96 Jacques Derrida, 'I'm Going to Have to Wander All Alone', *The Work of Mourning*, ed. Pascale-Anne Brault and Michael Naas (Chicago, IL, 2001), p. 192.

97 Ibid., p. 193.

98 Stivale, *Gilles Deleuze's ABCs*, p. 81.

99 Derrida, 'I'm Going to Have to Wander All Alone', p. 192.

100 Deleuze and Parnet, *Dialogues II*, p. 6.

101 'Toutes ces bêtises'. Deleuze, *Lettres et autres textes*, p. 61.

102 Gilles Deleuze and Félix Guattari, *Anti-Oedipus: Capitalism and Schizophrenia*, trans. Robert Hurley, Mark Seem and Helen R. Lane (Minneapolis, MN, 2005), p. 363.

103 Daniel W. Smith, 'The Inverse Side of the Structure: Žižek on Deleuze on Lacan', *Criticism*, XLIV/4 (2004), p. 648.

104 Lacan's positive response to Deleuze, including Deleuze's story of his encounter with Lacan is discussed in Smith, 'The Inverse Side of the Structure', p. 636.

105 For a clear overview, see Eugene Holland, 'Desire', in *Gilles Deleuze: Key Concepts*, ed. Charles J. Stivale, 2nd edn (Durham, 2011), p. 56.

106 Deleuze and Guattari, *Anti-Oedipus*, p. 26.

4 A Practice

 1 Deleuze, cited in 'Translators' Introduction', in Gilles Deleuze, *Cinema 1: The Movement-image*, trans. Hugh Tomlinson and Barbara Habberjam (London and New York, 1986), pp. xv–xvi.

 2 François Dosse, *Gilles Deleuze and Félix Guattari: Intersecting Lives*, trans. Deborah Glassman (New York, 2010), p. 90.

 3 Gilles Deleuze and Claire Parnet, *Dialogues II*, trans. Hugh Tomlinson and Barbara Habberjam (New York, 2007), p. 74.

 4 Gilles Deleuze, *Cinema 2: The Time-image*, trans. Hugh Tomlinson and Robert Galeta (Minneapolis, MN, 1989), p. 280.

 5 Gilles Deleuze and Félix Guattari, *What is Philosophy?*, trans. Graham Burchell and Hugh Tomlinson (London, 1994), p. 164.

 6 Gilles Deleuze, *Lettres et autres textes*, ed. David Lapoujade (Paris, 2015), p. 65.

 7 Gilles Deleuze, *Francis Bacon: The Logic of Sensation*, trans. Daniel W. Smith (London and New York, 2003), pp. 160–61.

 8 Alain Badiou and Barbara Cassin, 'Preface to the French Edition', in Deleuze, *Francis Bacon*, p. viii.

 9 See Dosse, *Gilles Deleuze and Félix Guattari*, p. 405.

10 Ibid., p. 441.

11 Gilles Deleuze, 'Hot and Cool', trans. Teal Eich, in *Desert Islands and Other Texts, 1953–1974*, ed. David Lapoujade, trans. Michael Taormina (New York, 2004), p. 247. Reprinted with this title in this posthumous collection of Deleuze's early texts, 'Hot and Cool' was originally written for the catalogue of an exhibition by Fromanger entitled *Fromanger, le peintre et le modele* (Paris, 1973).

12 Dosse, *Gilles Deleuze and Félix Guattari*, p. 441. 'Alors, il ne s'agit pas de noircir la toile mais de la blanchir . . .'; François Dosse, *Gilles Deleuze et Félix Guattari: Biographie Croisée* (Paris, 2007), p. 520.

13 Deleuze and Guattari, *What is Philosophy?*, p. 204.

14 Deleuze, *Francis Bacon*, p. 160. On Deleuze's Bacon book and the
    concept of sensation, see Jennifer Daryl Slack, 'The Logic of Sensation',
    in *Gilles Deleuze: Key Concepts*, ed. Charles J. Stivale (Durham, 2011).

15 Claire Colebrook, *Gilles Deleuze* (London and New York, 2002), p. 38.

16 Deleuze, *Cinema 2*, p. 25.

17 Ibid., p. xi.

18 Gilles Deleuze, *Negotiations*, trans. Martin Joughin (New York, 1995),
    pp. 38–9.

19 'C'est d'une grande médiocrité, il faut qu'on mêle.' Deleuze, *Lettres et
    autres textes*, p. 55.

20 In a 1982 letter to Arnaud Villani, Deleuze writes that he dreams of
    writing but that he miscalculated and the cinema course has caused
    more worries and work than he anticipated ('Mon rêve, ce serait
    d'écrire, mais de ne pus parler du tout. Je me suis flanqué cette année
    dans un cours sur le cinéma, tel que je pensais avoir une année sans
    peine, et il se révèle que jamais un cours ne m'a donné plus de souci
    et de préparation. J'ai raté mon calcul.') Ibid.

21 Literary references also recur with considerable frequency in his
    work with Guattari. Their *A Thousand Plateaus*, Ronald Bogue notes,
    contains references to more than 75 different writers. Ronald Bogue,
    Deleuze on Literature (London and New York, 2003), p. 1.

22 Deleuze, *Negotiations*, p. 100.

23 Ibid., p. 143.

24 Gilles Deleuze, *Masochism: Coldness and Cruelty*, trans. Jean McNeil
    (New York, 1991), pp. 13–14.

25 Gregg Lambert, 'On the Uses and Abuses of Literature for Life:
    Gilles Deleuze and the Literary Clinic', *Postmodern Culture*, VIII/3,
    1998), para. 1.

26 Gilles Deleuze, *Essays Critical and Clinical*, trans. Daniel W. Smith
    and Michael A. Greco (Minneapolis, MN, 1997), p. 141.

27 Gilles Deleuze, *Proust and Signs: The Complete Text*, trans. Richard
    Howard (London and New York, 2008), p. 59.

28 Deleuze and Parnet, *Dialogues II*, p. 74.

29 Deleuze, *Essays Critical and Clinical*, p. 4.

30 Deleuze, *Negotiations*, p. 128.

31 Deleuze and Parnet, *Dialogues II*, p. 74.

32 Deleuze, *Negotiations*, p. 100.

33 Deleuze, *Essays Critical and Clinical*, p. 4.

34 Gilles Deleuze and Félix Guattari, *Kafka: Toward a Minor Literature*, trans. Dana Polan (Minneapolis, MN, 1986), pp. 16–18.

35 Ibid., p. 26.

36 Ronald Bogue, *Deleuze on Music, Painting, and the Arts* (London and New York, 2003), pp. 2–3.

37 'Si l'on pouvait faire de la galopade et de la ritournelle deux complémentaires, cela m'arrangerait beaucoup.' Deleuze, *Lettres et autres textes*, pp. 24–5.

38 Deleuze and Guattari, *A Thousand Plateaus: Capitalism and Schizophrenia*, trans. Brian Massumi (London and New York, 2004), p. 343.

39 Ian Buchanan, 'Introduction', in *Deleuze and Music*, ed. Ian Buchanan and Marcel Swiboda (Edinburgh, 2004), p. 16.

40 For a useful explication and deployment of Deleuze on music, see Bogue's *Deleuze on Music, Painting, and the Arts*.

41 Deleuze, *Negotiations*, p. 137.

42 Ibid., p. 125.

43 Dosse, *Gilles Deleuze and Félix Guattari*, p. 444.

44 Mark Bonta and John Protevi, *Deleuze and Geophilosophy* (Edinburgh, 2004), p. 12.

45 Alan D. Schrift, *Twentieth-century French Philosophy: Key Themes and Thinkers* (Malden, MA, and Oxford, 2006), pp. 75–8.

46 Gilles Deleuze and Claire Parnet, *L'Abécédaire de Gilles Deleuze*, dir. Pierre-André Boutang (Video Editions Montparnasse, 1988–9), 'M comme maladie'.

47 Deleuze, *Negotiations*, p. 137.

48 Ibid., p. 136.

49 François Cusset, *French Theory: How Foucault, Derrida, Deleuze, & Co. Transformed the Intellectual Life of the United States* (Minneapolis, MN, 2008), pp. 67–8. Cusset's description of the meeting with the 1960s iconic singers is funny and illustrative enough to warrant inclusion here: 'He took them to see Ginsberg at his apartment on Tenth Street and then to a concert in Massachusetts where Deleuze and Guattari met Bob Dylan and Joan Baez – but the latter hadn't read *Anti-Oedipus*, and the former weren't all that into smoking pot.'

50 Ibid., pp. 69–70.

51 Dosse, *Gilles Deleuze and Félix Guattari*, p. 471.
52 Deleuze and Parnet, *Dialogues II*, pp. 36–7.
53 Cusset, *French Theory*, p. 282.
54 Alice Jardine, 'Woman in Limbo: Deleuze and his (Br)others',
    SubStance, XIII/3–4, issue 44–5: *Gilles Deleuze* (1984), p. 54. The
    article appears subsequently in Jardine's book *Gynesis: Configurations
    of Woman and Identity* (Ithaca, NY, 1986). For an alternative and
    summative view of Deleuze's 'becoming-woman', see Patty Sotirin,
    'Becoming-woman', in *Gilles Deleuze: Key Concepts*, ed. Charles J.
    Stivale, 2nd edn (Durham, NC, 2011).
55 Deleuze and Parnet, *Dialogues II*, p. 7.

5 A Life

1 Gilles Deleuze, *Negotiations*, trans. Martin Joughin (New York, 1995),
   p. 143.
2 Laura Cull, 'Deleuze, Philosophical Diseases and the Thought of
   Illness', *Philosophy on Stage*, 3, n.p., http://homepage.univie.ac.at/
   arno.boehler/php/?p=5360, accessed 11 November 2016.
3 François Dosse, *Gilles Deleuze and Félix Guattari: Intersecting Lives*,
   trans. Deborah Glassman (New York, 2010), p. 178.
4 Gilles Deleuze, *Lettres et autres textes*, ed. David Lapoujade (Paris, 2015),
   p. 58.
5 'A song rises, approaches, or fades away. That's what it's like on the
   plane of immanence: multiplicities fill it, singularities connect with
   one another, processes or becomings unfold, intensities rise and fall.'
   Deleuze, *Negotiations*, pp. 146–7.
6 Gilles Deleuze and Claire Parnet, *Dialogues II*, trans. Hugh Tomlinson
   and Barbara Habberjam (New York, 2007), p. 5.
7 See the chapter 'Active and Reactive', in Deleuze's *Nietzsche and
   Philosophy*, trans. Hugh Tomlinson (London and New York, 2006).
   See also Kenneth Surin, 'Force', in *Gilles Deleuze: Key Concepts*,
   ed. Charles J. Stivale, 2nd edn (Durham, 2011).
8 Gilles Deleuze, *Nietzsche and Philosophy*, trans. Hugh Tomlinson
   (London and New York, 2006), p. 3.
9 Deleuze, *Lettres et autres textes*, p. 52.

10 Gilles Deleuze, 'Proust Round Table', in Deleuze, *Two Regimes of Madness: Texts and Interviews, 1975–1995*, ed. David Lapoujade, trans. Ames Hodges and Mike Taormina (New York, 2007), p. 41.

11 See Gilles Deleuze, 'Nineteenth Series of Humor', in Deleuze, *The Logic of Sense*, trans. Mark Lester with Charles Stivale, ed. Constantin V. Boundas (London and New York, 2004), pp. 153–61.

12 Charles J. Stivale, *Gilles Deleuze's ABCs: The Folds of Friendship* (Baltimore, MD, 2008), p. 118.

13 Ibid., p. 122.

14 Deleuze and Parnet, *Dialogues II*, p. 5.

15 'C'est ce qui me dégoûte, théoriquement, pratiquement, toute espèce de plainte à l'égard de la vie, toute culture tragique.' Deleuze, *Lettres et autres textes*, p. 78.

16 Deleuze and Parnet, *Dialogues II*, p. 6.

17 Friedrich Nietzsche, *The Gay Science: With a Prelude in Rhymes and an Appendix of Songs*, trans. Walter Kaufmann (New York, 1974), section 382.

18 Deleuze in Gilles Deleuze and Claire Parnet, *Gilles Deleuze from A to Z*, trans Charles J. Stivale (Cambridge and New York, 2012), 'O as in Opera'.

19 Deleuze, *Negotiations*, p. 143.

20 Gilles Deleuze, 'Literature and Life', in Deleuze, *Essays Critical and Clinical*, trans. Daniel W. Smith and Michael A. Greco (Minneapolis, MN, 1997), pp. 3–4.

21 Here, again, we need to evoke the concept of the body as constituted simply by various organic parts. Experience, for Deleuze, emerges through a whole spectrum of organic as well as nonorganic events and expressions. The subject is not an entity that transcends and precedes its environment but rather a temporary and mutable effect of a whole range of expressions of life, not all of which can be accounted for within traditional notions of the organic and the human. Similarly, the body is not a fixed entity but one that emerges in conjunction with organic as well as nonorganic entities, with animals, plants, music or painting.

22 Deleuze, *Negotiations*, p. 11.

23 Gilles Deleuze, *The Logic of Sense*, trans. Mark Lester and Charles Stivale, ed Constantin V. Boundas (London and New York, 2004), pp. 4–5.

24 Deleuze and Parnet, *Dialogues II*, pp. 64–5.

25 Ibid., p. 65.

26 See for example Deleuze and Parnet, *Dialogues II*, p. 12, and Deleuze and Guattari, *Anti-Oedipus*, p. 2.

27 In their book on Kafka, Deleuze and Guattari also quite explicitly reject metaphor in favour of metamorphosis. Noting how Kafka 'deliberately kills all metaphor', they see this as entailing the exchange of proper sense for intensities and deterritorializations. Gilles Deleuze and Félix Guattari, *Kafka: Toward a Minor Literature*, trans. Dana Polan (Minneapolis, MN, 1986), p. 22.

28 Gilles Deleuze, *Pure Immanence: Essays on a Life*, trans. Anne Boyman (New York, 2001), pp. 28–9.

29 Deleuze, in *Gilles Deleuze from A to Z*, 'M as in Malady'.

30 'Ma santé devient plus mauvaise, ou plutôt ce n'est pas de la maladie, c'est un état qui fait que j'ai de la peine à respirer, constamment: vous ne vous doutez pas à quel point ça change toute chose, y compris dans le travail.' Deleuze, *Lettres et autres textes*, p. 87.

31 Deleuze, cited in Dosse, *Gilles Deleuze and Félix Guattari*, p. 497.

32 Lebel in interview with Virginie Linhart, cited in Dosse, *Gilles Deleuze and Félix Guattari*, p. 497.

33 Dosse, *Gilles Deleuze and Félix Guattari*, pp. 497–8.

34 Ibid., p. 498.

35 Deleuze, in *Gilles Deleuze from A to Z*, 'B as in Boire'.

36 Dosse, *Gilles Deleuze and Félix Guattari*, p. 351.

37 'Je poursuis la version definitive de *Qu'est-ce que la philosophie?* moins comme un oiseau inspiré que comme un âne qui se frappe lui-même.' Deleuze, *Lettres et autres textes*, p. 97.

38 Gilles Deleuze, *Essays Critical and Clinical*, trans. Daniel W. Smith and Michael A. Greco (Minneapolis, MN, 1997), p. 152.

39 Ibid.

40 Ibid., p. 155.

41 In an interview with Dosse, Noelle Châtelet recalls receiving a letter from Deleuze two weeks before his death in which he writes that he did not want to go through what François had gone through. Dosse, *Gilles Deleuze and Félix Guattari*, p. 497.

42 Gilles Deleuze, *Difference and Repetition*, trans. Paul Patton (London and New York, 2004), pp. 322–3.

43 Deleuze, in *Gilles Deleuze from A to Z*, 'R as in Resistance'.

44 'A Gilles Deleuze, l'inventeur, l'innocent, le rieur, le fugueur: l'adieu des philosophes', *Libération*, 7 November 1995, n.p.

45 'Nous reprendrons la tâche.' Jean-Luc Nancy, 'De sens, dans tous les sens', *Libération*, 7 November 1995, n.p.

46 'C'est ton chagrin idiot, dit-il.' Jean-François Lyotard, 'Il était la bibliotèque de Babel', *Libération*, 7 November 1995, n.p.

47 'Ce n'est pas le petit plaisir d'être soi . . . cette contemplation des réquisits propres qui produit la joie, la naïve confiance que ça va durer, sans laquelle on ne pourrait pas vivre, car le coeur s'arrêterait.' Giorgio Agamben, 'Sauf les hommes et les chiens', *Libération*, 7 November 1995, n.p.

48 'Trop à dire, oui, sur le temps qu'avec tant d'autres de ma <<génération>> il m'a été donné de partager avec Deleuze, sur la chance de penser grâce à lui, en pensant à lui.' Jacques Derrida, 'I'm Going to Have to Wander All Alone', *The Work of Mourning*, ed. Pascale-Anne Brault and Michael Naas (Chicago, IL, 2001), p. 192.

49 John Rajchman, 'Introduction', in Deleuze, *Pure Immanence*, p. 20.

50 Deleuze, *Pure Immanence*, p. 29.

Conclusion

1 Gilles Deleuze and Claire Parnet, *Dialogues II*, trans. Hugh Tomlinson and Barbara Habberjam (New York, 2007), p. 5.

2 'De le retenir en tant que "lui-même", de faire un "arrêt sur image".' Jean-Luc Nancy, 'De sens, dans tous les sens', *Libération*, 7 November 1995, n.p.

3 Ibid.

4 Gilles Deleuze and Félix Guattari, *A Thousand Plateaus: Capitalism and Schizophrenia*, trans. Brian Massumi (London and New York, 2004), p. 13.

5 'J'ai vu des cas de gens qui voulaient bien se faire le "disciple" de quelqu'un, et qui avaient certes autant de talent que le "maître", mais

qui en sortaient stérilisés. C'est terrible. Travailler sur moi a deux inconvénients majeurs pour vous: ça ne vous aidera pas dans votre carrière universitaire, ce qui n'est peut-être pas l'essentiel, mais est quand même très important; et surtout vous avez à faire votre propre œuvre poétique et philosophique, qui ne peut pas supporter d'être contrainte par la mienne.' Gilles Deleuze, *Lettres et autres textes*, ed. David Lapoujade (Paris, 2015), p. 80.

6 Constantin V. Boundas, 'Introduction', in *Gilles Deleuze: The Intensive Reduction*, ed. Boundas (London and New York, 2009), p. 1.

7 Elie During, 'Blackboxing in Theory: Deleuze versus Deleuze', in *French Theory in America*, ed. Sylvère Lotringer and Sande Cohen (London and New York, 2001), p. 165.

8 Ibid.

9 Eleanor Kaufman, 'Betraying Well', *Criticism*, XLVI/4 (2004), p. 651.

10 Ibid., p. 652.

11 During, 'Blackboxing in Theory', p. 170.

12 Ibid., pp. 166–7.

13 Kaufman, 'Betraying Well', p. 651.

14 Daniel W. Smith, 'The Inverse Side of the Structure: Žižek on Deleuze on Lacan', *Criticism*, XLVI/4 (2004), p. 637.

15 Elizabeth A. Grosz, *Volatile Bodies: Toward a Corporeal Feminism* (Bloomington, IN, 1994), p. 180.

16 Rosi Braidotti, *Nomadic Subjects: Embodiment and Sexual Difference in Contemporary Feminist Theory* (New York, 2013), p. 123.

17 'Un rapport énonçable', Deleuze, *Lettres et autres textes*, p. 77.

18 Deleuze and Guattari, *A Thousand Plateaus*, p. 307.

19 See, for example Luciana Parisi's *Abstract Sex: Philosophy, Bio-technology and the Mutations of Desire* (London and New York, 2004), and Claire Colebrook, *Sex After Life: Essays on Extinction*, vol. II (Ann Arbor, MI, 2014).

20 Slavoj Žižek, *Organs Without Bodies: On Deleuze and Consequences* (London and New York, 2012), p. 18.

21 Smith, 'The Inverse Side of the Structure', p. 638.

22 Žižek, *Organs Without Bodies*, p. 18.

23 Ibid., p. 163.

24 Peter Hallward, *Out of this World: Deleuze and the Philosophy of Creation* (London, 2006), p. 162.

25 I am referring here to Michael Hardt and Antonio Negri's *Empire* (2000), *Multitude* (2004) and *Commonwealth* (2009).

26 For the relation between Foucault's and Deleuze's understandings of biopower, see for example Paul Patton, 'Activism, Philosophy and Actuality in Deleuze and Foucault', *Deleuze Studies*, IV/10: *Deleuze and Political Activism*, ed. Marcelo Svirsky (2010), pp. 84–103.

27 See Nicolae Morar, Thomas Nail and Daniel W. Smith, 'Introduction', in *Foucault Studies*, 17 (2014), pp. 4–10. The transcripts and recordings can be found at www2.univ-paris8.fr/deleuze/rubrique.php3?id_rubrique=21, accessed 13 December 2016.

28 Rosi Braidotti and Rick Dolphijn, eds, *This Deleuzian Century: Art, Activism, Life* (Leiden, 2014), pp. 13, 34.

29 Marcelo Svirsky, 'Introduction: Beyond the Royal Science of Politics', in *Deleuze Studies*, IV/10: *Deleuze and Political Activism*, ed. Marcelo Svirsky (2010), p. 5.

30 Ibid., p. 3.

31 Ibid., p. 4.

32 Deleuze and Parnet, *Dialogues II*, p. 147.

33 Quoted in Eyal Weizman, *Hollow Land: Israel's Architecture of Occupation* (London, 2012), pp. 200–201.

34 Shimon Naveh, 'Between the Striated and the Smooth: Asymmetric Warfare, Operational Art, and Alternative Learning Strategies', *Counter Insurgency*, conference at the Swedish Defence University (org. Dan Öberg), Stockholm, 5–6 November 2007. In Deleuze and Guattari's original this reads, 'deterritorialize the enemy by shattering his territory from within' (*A Thousand Plateaus*, p. 390).

35 Eyal Weizman, 'Walking through Walls: Soldier as Architects in the Israeli–Palestinian Conflict', *Radical Philosophy*, 136 (2006), p. 8.

36 Quoted in During, 'Blackboxing in Theory', p. 167.

37 Deleuze, *Negotiations*, p. 89.

38 John Rajchman, *The Deleuze Connections* (Cambridge, MA, and London, 2000), p. 75.

Bibliography

Texts by Gilles Deleuze

'Description de la femme. Pour une philosophie d'autrui sexuée', *Poésie*,
    XLV/28 (October–November 1945), pp. 28–39
Empirisme et subjectivité (1953)
—, *Empiricism and Subjectivity*, trans. Constantin Boundas (New York, 1991)
Nietzsche et la philosophie (1962)
—, *Nietzsche and Philosophy*, trans. Hugh Tomlinson (London and
    New York, 2006)
La Philosophie critique de Kant (Paris, 1963)
—, *The Critical Philosophy of Kant*, trans. Hugh Tomlinson and Barbara
    Habberjam (Minneapolis, MN, 1984)
Proust et les signes (Paris, 1964, 1970, 1976)
—, *Proust and Signs: The Complete Text*, trans. Richard Howard
    (London and New York, 2008)
Le Bergsonisme (Paris, 1966)
—, *Bergsonism*, trans. Hugh Tomlinson and Barbara Habberjam
    (New York, 1988)
Présentation de Sacher-Masoch (Paris, 1967)
—, *Masochism: Coldness and Cruelty*, trans. Jean McNeil
    (New York, 1991)
Différence et répétition (Paris, 1968)
—, *Difference and Repetition*, trans. Paul Patton (London and
    New York, 2004)
Spinoza et le problème de l'expression (Paris, 1968)
—, *Expressionism in Philosophy: Spinoza*, trans. Martin Joughin
    (New York, 1990)

Logique du sens (Paris, 1969)

—, *The Logic of Sense*, ed. Constantin V. Boundas, trans. Mark Lester
   with Charles Stivale (London and New York, 2004)

Spinoza: Philosophie pratique (Paris, 1970/1981)

—, *Spinoza: Practical Philosophy*, trans. Robert Hurley
   (San Francisco, CA, 1988)

Francis Bacon: Logique de la sensation (Paris, 1981)

—, *Francis Bacon: The Logic of Sensation*, trans. Daniel W. Smith
   (London and New York, 2003)

Cinéma 1: L'Image-mouvement (Paris, 1983)

—, *Cinema 1: The Movement-image*, trans. Hugh Tomlinson
   and Barbara Habberjam (London and New York, 1986)

—, *Cinema 1: The Movement-image*, trans. Hugh Tomlinson
   and Barbara Habberjam (London and New York, 2005)

Cinéma 2: L'Image-temps (Paris, 1985)

—, *Cinema 2: The Time-image*, trans. Hugh Tomlinson and Robert Galeta
   (Minneapolis, MN, 1989)

Foucault (Paris, 1986)

—, *Foucault*, trans. Seán Hand (London and New York, 2006)

Le Pli: Leibniz et le baroque (Paris, 1988)

—, *The Fold: Leibniz and the Baroque*, trans. Tom Conley
   (Minneapolis, MN, 1993)

Pourparlers (Paris, 1990)

—, *Negotiations*, trans. Martin Joughin (New York, 1995)

Critique et Clinique (Paris, 1993)

—, *Essays Critical and Clinical*, trans. Daniel W. Smith and Michael A.
   Greco (Minneapolis, MN, 1997)

'L'Immanence: une vie' (Paris, 1995)

—, 'Immanence: A Life', in *Two Regimes of Madness: Texts and Interviews,
   1975–1995*, ed. David Lapoujade, trans. Ames Hodges and Mike
   Taormina (New York, 2007)

Pure Immanence: Essays on a Life, trans. Anne Boyman
   (New York, 2001)

L'Île déserte et autres textes: Textes et entretiens, 1953–1974 (Paris, 2002)

—, *Desert Islands and Other Texts, 1953–1974*, ed. David Lapoujade,
   trans. Michael Taormina (New York, 2004)

Deux régimes de fous: Textes et entretiens, 1975–1995 (Paris, 2003)

—, *Two Regimes of Madness: Texts and Interviews, 1975–1995*, ed. David
    Lapoujade, trans. Ames Hodges and Mike Taormina (New York, 2007)
Lettres et autres textes, ed. David Lapoujade (Paris, 2015)

With Félix Guattari

L'Anti-Œdipe (Paris, 1972)
—, *Anti-Oedipus: Capitalism and Schizophrenia*, trans. Robert Hurley,
    Mark Seem and Helen R. Lane (Minneapolis, MN, 2005)
Kafka: Pour une littérature mineure (Paris, 1975)
—, *Kafka: Toward a Minor Literature*, trans. Dana Polan (Minneapolis,
    MN, 1986)
Mille plateaux (Paris, 1980)
—, *A Thousand Plateaus: Capitalism and Schizophrenia*, trans. Brian
    Massumi (London and New York, 2004)
Qu'est-ce que la philosophie? (Paris, 1991)
—, *What is Philosophy?*, trans. Graham Burchell and Hugh Tomlinson
    (London, 1994)

With Claire Parnet

Dialogues (Paris, 1977)
—, *Dialogues II*, trans. Hugh Tomlinson and Barbara Habberjam
    (New York, 2007)
L'Abécédaire de Gilles Deleuze, directed by Pierre-André Boutang,
    Video Editions Montparnasse (1988–9)
—, *Gilles Deleuze from A to Z*, DVD, trans. Charles J. Stivale
    (Cambridge and New York, 2011)

Secondary Sources

'A Gilles Deleuze, l'inventeur, l'innocent, le rieur, le fugueur:
    l'adieu des philosophes', *Libération*, 7 November 1995,
    www.liberation.fr

Agamben, Giorgio, 'Sauf les hommes et les chiens', *Libération*, 7 November, www.liberation.fr

Arendt, Hannah, 'Heidegger at Eighty', in *Heidegger and Modern Philosophy: Critical Essays*, ed. Michael Murray (New Haven, CT, and London, 1978), pp. 293–303

Badiou, Alain, *Deleuze: The Clamor of Being*, trans. Louise Burchill (Minneapolis, MN, 2000)

—, and Barbara Cassin, 'Preface to the French Edition', in Gilles Deleuze, *Francis Bacon: The Logic of Sensation*, trans. Daniel W. Smith (London and New York, 2003), p. vii

Barthes, Roland, 'The Death of the Author', in *Image – Music – Text*, trans. and ed. Stephen Heath (London, 1977), pp. 142–8

Baudrillard, Jean, *Forget Foucault*, trans. Nicole Dufresne, Phil Beitchman, Lee Hildreth and Mark Polizzotri (New York, 1987)

Beckman, Frida, *Between Desire and Pleasure: A Deleuzian Theory of Sexuality* (Edinburgh, 2013)

Bergen, Véronique, 'Deleuze and the Question of Ontology', in *Gilles Deleuze: The Intensive Reduction*, ed. Constantin V. Boundas (London and New York, 2009), pp. 7–22

Bianco, Giuseppe, *Après Bergson: Portrait de groupe avec philosophe* (Paris, 2015)

Bogue, Ronald, *Deleuze on Literature* (London and New York, 2003)

—, *Deleuze on Music, Painting, and the Arts* (London and New York, 2003)

Boundas, Constantin V., 'Introduction', in *Gilles Deleuze: The Intensive Reduction*, ed. Constantin V. Boundas (London and New York, 2009)

Braidotti, Rosi, and Rick Dolphijn, eds, *This Deleuzian Century: Art, Activism, Life* (Leiden, 2014)

—, *Nomadic Subjects: Embodiment and Sexual Difference in Contemporary Feminist Theory* (New York, 2013)

Buchanan, Ian, and Marcel Swiboda, eds, *Deleuze and Music* (Edinburgh, 2004)

—, and Nicholas Thoburn, 'Introduction: Deleuze and Politics', in *Deleuze and Politics* (Edinburgh, 2008), pp. 1–12

Colebrook, Claire, *Gilles Deleuze* (London and New York, 2002)

—, *Sex After Life: Essays on Extinction*, vol. II (Ann Arbor, MI, 2014)

Collapse, vol. III: *Unknown Deleuze [+ Speculative Realism]*, ed. Robin Mackay (2012)

Conley, Tom, 'Translator's Foreword: A Plea for Leibniz', in *The Fold: Leibniz and the Baroque* (Minneapolis, MN, 1993), pp. ix–xx.

Cull, Laura, 'Deleuze, Philosophical Diseases and the Thought of Illness', *Philosophy on Stage*, 3, http://homepage.univie.ac.at/arno.boehler/php/?p=5360, accessed 30 August 2016

Cusset, François, *French Theory: How Foucault, Derrida, Deleuze, & Co. Transformed the Intellectual Life of the United States*, trans. Jeff Ford with Josephine Berganza and Marlon Jones (Minneapolis, MN, 2008)

Delpech-Ramey, Joshua, 'Deleuze, Guattari, and the "Politics of Sorcery"', *SubStance*, XXXIX/1, issue 121: *Spiritual Politics after Deleuze* (2010), pp. 8–23

Derrida, Jacques, 'I'm Going to Have to Wander All Alone', in *The Work of Mourning*, ed. Pascale-Anne Brault and Michael Naas (Chicago, IL, 2001), pp. 189–95

Dosse, François, *Gilles Deleuze et Félix Guattari: Biographie croisée* (Paris, 2007)

—, *Gilles Deleuze and Félix Guattari: Intersecting Lives*, trans. Deborah Glassman (New York, 2010)

During, Elie, 'Blackboxing in Theory: Deleuze versus Deleuze', in *French Theory in America*, ed. Sylvère Lotringer and Sande Cohen (London and New York, 2001)

Ewald, François, 'Editorial Foreword: Desire and Pleasure, Gilles Deleuze', trans. Melissa McMahon, 1997 (www.artdes.monash.edu.au/globe/delfou.html#1, accessed 30 August 2016). Originally published as 'Désir et plaisir', *Magazine littéraire*, 325 (October 1994), pp. 59–65

Flaxman, Gregory, *Gilles Deleuze and the Fabulation of Philosophy* (Minneapolis, MN, 2012)

Foucault, Michel, *Language, Counter-memory, Practice: Selected Essays and Interviews*, ed. Donald F. Bouchard (New York, 1977)

—, 'What is an Author?', in *Essential Works of Foucault, 1954–1984*, vol. II: *Aesthetics, Method, and Epistemology*, ed. James D. Faubion, trans. Robert Hurley et al. (New York, 1998), pp. 205–22

Grosz, Elizabeth A., *Volatile Bodies: Toward a Corporeal Feminism* (Bloomington, IN, 1994)

Guattari, Félix, *The Anti-Oedipus Papers*, ed. Stéphane Nadaud, trans. Kélina Gotman (New York, 2006)

Hallward, Peter, *Out of this World: Deleuze and the Philosophy of Creation* (London, 2006)

Hardt, Michael, *Gilles Deleuze: An Apprenticeship in Philosophy*
(Minneapolis, MN, 1993)
Hardt, Michael, and Antonio Negri, *Commonwealth*
(Cambridge, MA, and London, 2009)
—, *Empire* (Cambridge, MA, and London, 2000)
—, *Multitude: War and Democracy in the Age of Empire* (New York, 2004)
Hickey-Moody, Anna Catherine, 'Deleuze's Children', *Educational
Philosophy and Theory*, XLV/3 (2013), pp. 272–86
Holland, Eugene, 'Desire', in *Gilles Deleuze: Key Concepts*, ed. Charles J.
Stivale (Durham, 2011), pp. 55–64
Jardine, Alice, *Gynesis: Configurations of Woman and Identity*
(Ithaca, NY, 1986)
—, 'Woman in Limbo: Deleuze and his (Br)others', *SubStance*, XIII/3–4,
issue 44–5: *Gilles Deleuze* (1984), pp. 46–60
Kaufman, Eleanor, 'Betraying Well', *Criticism*, XLVI/4 (2004), pp. 651–9
—, *The Delirium of Praise: Bataille, Blanchot, Deleuze, Foucault, Klossowski*
(Baltimore, MD, 2001)
Kerslake, Christian, *Deleuze and the Unconscious* (London and
New York, 2007)
Lambert, Gregg, 'On the Uses and Abuses of Literature for Life:
Gilles Deleuze and the Literary Clinic', *Postmodern Culture*, VIII/3
(1998), n.p.
—, *Who's Afraid of Deleuze and Guattari?* (London and New York, 2006)
Lapoujade, David, 'Introduction', in Gilles Deleuze, *Desert Islands and
Other Texts, 1953–1974*, ed. David Lapoujade, trans. Michael Taormina
(New York, 2004), p. 7
Lyotard, Jean-François, 'Il était la bibliotèque de Babel', *Libération*,
7 November 1995, www.liberation.fr
Marks, John, *Gilles Deleuze: Vitalism and Multiplicity* (London, 1998)
Massumi, Brian, *A User's Guide to Capitalism and Schizophrenia:
Deviations from Deleuze and Guattari* (Cambridge, MA, and
London, 1992)
Morar, Nicolae, Thomas Nail and Daniel W. Smith, 'Introduction',
Foucault Studies, 17 (2014), pp. 4–10
Nail, Thomas, 'Review', *Foucault Studies*, XIV (2012), pp. 218–22
Nancy, Jean-Luc, 'Du sens, dans tous les sens', *Libération*, 7 November 1995,
www.liberation.fr

Naveh, Shimon, 'Between the Striated and the Smooth: Asymmetric Warfare, Operational Art, and Alternative Learning Strategies', *Counter Insurgency*, conference at the Swedish Defense College (org. Dan Öberg), Stockholm, 5–6 November 2007

Nietzsche, Friedrich, *The Gay Science: With a Prelude in Rhymes and an Appendix of Songs*, trans. Walter Kaufmann (New York, 1974)

—, *The Gay Science*, trans. R. J. Hollingdale (New York, 1989)

—, *On the Genealogy of Morals* and *Ecce Homo*, ed. and trans. Walter Kaufmann (New York, 1989)

—, *Thus Spoke Zarathustra*, trans. Thomas Common (Raleigh, NC, 1999)

Osborne, Peter, 'Guattareze?', *New Left Review*, LXIV (2011), pp. 139–51

Parisi, Luciana, *Abstract Sex: Philosophy, Bio-Technology and the Mutations of Desire* (London and New York, 2004)

Patton, Paul, 'Activism, Philosophy and Actuality in Deleuze and Foucault', *Deleuze Studies*, IV/10: *Deleuze and Political Activism*, ed. Marcelo Svirsky (2010), pp. 84–103

—, ed., *Deleuze and the Political* (London, 2000), pp. 1–10

Pavlov, Evgeni V., 'The Banality of Genius: When Deleuze Met Guattari', *Parallax*, XVIII/1 (2012), pp. 112–16

Peeters, Benoît, *Derrida: A Biography*, trans. Andrew Brown (Cambridge, 2013)

Rajchman, John, *The Deleuze Connections* (Cambridge, MA, and London, 2000)

—, 'Introduction', in Gilles Deleuze, *Pure Immanence: Essays on a Life*, trans. Anne Boyman (New York, 2001), pp. 7–23

Ramey, Joshua, *The Hermetic Deleuze: Philosophy and the Spiritual Ordeal* (Durham, NC, and London, 2012)

Rancière, Jacques, 'Is there a Deleuzian Aesthetics?', trans. Radmila Djordjevic, *Qui Parle*, XIV/2 (2004), pp. 1–14

Schrift, Alan D., 'The Effects on the *Agrégation de Philosophie* on Twentieth-century French Philosophy', *Journal of the History of Philosophy*, XLVI/3, 2008, pp. 449–73

—, 'French Nietzscheanism', *Poststructuralism and Critical Theory's Second Generation*, vol. VI of *The History of Continental Philosophy*, ed. Alan D. Schrift (London and New York, 2014), pp. 19–46

—, 'Intersecting Lives', *Symploke*, XX/1–2 (2012), pp. 341–4

—, *Twentieth-century French Philosophy: Key Themes and Thinkers* (Malden, MA, and Oxford, 2006)

Slack, Jennifer Daryl, 'The Logic of Sensation', in *Gilles Deleuze: Key Concepts*, ed, Charles J. Stivale, 2nd edn (Durham, NC, 2011), pp. 153–62

Smith, Daniel W., 'Gilles Deleuze', in *Poststructuralism and Critical Theory's Second Generation*, vol. VI of *The History of Continental Philosophy*, ed. Alan D. Schrift (London and New York, 2014), pp. 91–110

—, 'Introduction: "A Life of Pure Immanence": Deleuze's "Critique et Clinique" Project', in Gilles Deleuze, *Essays Critical and Clinical*, trans. Daniel W. Smith and Michael A. Greco (Minneapolis, MN, 1997), pp. xi–lvi

—, 'The Inverse Side of the Structure: Žižek on Deleuze on Lacan', *Criticism*, XLVI/4 (2004), pp. 635–50

Sotirin, Patty, 'Becoming-woman', in *Gilles Deleuze: Key Concepts*, ed. Charles J. Stivale, 2nd edn (Durham, 2011), pp. 116–30

Stivale, Charles J., ed., *Gilles Deleuze: Key Concepts*, 2nd edn (Durham, 2011)

—, ed. *Gilles Deleuze's ABCs: The Folds of Friendship* (Baltimore, MD, 2008)

Surin, Kenneth, 'Force', in *Gilles Deleuze: Key Concepts*, ed. Charles J. Stivale, 2nd edn (Durham, 2011), pp. 21–32

Svirsky, Marcelo, 'Introduction: Beyond the Royal Science of Politics', *Deleuze Studies*, IV/10: *Deleuze and Political Activism* (2010), pp. 1–6

Tomlinson, Hugh, and Barbara Haberjam, 'Translators' Introduction', in *Dialogues II*, trans. Hugh Tomlinson and Barbara Habberjam (New York, 2007), pp. xi–xiii

Tournier, Michel, *The Wind Spirit: An Autobiography*, trans. Arthur Goldhammer (London, 1989)

Weizman, Eyal, *Hollow Land: Israel's Architecture of Occupation* (London, 2012)

—, 'Walking through Walls: Soldier as Architects in the Israeli–Palestinian Conflict', *Radical Philosophy*, 136 (2006), pp. 8–22

Žižek, Slavoj, *Organs Without Bodies: On Deleuze and Consequences* (London and New York, 2012)

Acknowledgements

I was mad to take on this project. I knew so when I accepted the invitation and I have been reminded of it repeatedly throughout the process. I would not and could not have done it without the fantastic support I received from several colleagues in the field. Charles J. Stivale helped me by believing in me from the beginning and by reading and responding to the first full version of the manuscript. Charley – it wouldn't have happened at all without you. Another Charles, Charlie Blake, read various parts of the text at various stages and provided enormous support throughout. Charlie – thank you as always. In this middle period, an anonymous reader of the manuscript also supplied very useful feedback. Finally, and towards the end, Alan D. Schrift generously took his time to communicate with me and also to read one of the final versions of the manuscript and provide crucial comments and suggestions. Alan – it is thanks to you that I finally found the courage to press 'send'. I have also had many formal as well as informal exchanges on the topic of this biography with friends and colleagues including Giuseppe Bianco, Gary Genosko, Joe Hughes, Gregg Lambert and Daniel W. Smith.

I would also like to extend a very warm thanks to two colleagues at the Department of English – Sarah Bouttier and Hanta Persson – for assisting me with the translations and covering up for my *pauvre* French – merci beaucoup! Pernilla Jansson was an invaluable assistant – and not for the first time. Finally, I would like to thank Ben Hayes at Reaktion Books for inviting me to write the book in the first place, and Martha Jay and Jess Chandler for helping me get it into shape.

A generous grant from Literature as a Leading Research Area at Stockholm University enabled me to secure copyright for the images included in the book.

Photo Acknowledgements

© Helen Bamberger/Cosmos/eyevine: p. 6; © Marc Gantier/Gamma-Rapho via Getty Images: p. 52; © Herve Gloaguen/Getty: p. 43; Ohira Hiromoto: p. 90; image courtesy of Joe Hughes: pp. 36, 83; © Elie Kagan/BDIC: p. 58; Thierry Larère, reprinted with permission, www.flickr.com/photos/clichesdeparlemonde: p. 14; © Jean-Jacques Lebel, ADAGP, Paris: pp. 96, 107; Sylvère Lotringer: p. 95; Courtesy of Musée l'Organe – Demeure du Chaos/Abode of Chaos, www.abodeofchaos.org, www.demeureduchaos.org: p. 123; © Gérard Uféras: p. 110; © archives Pontigny-Cerisy reproduction interdite: p. 73.